Happy Sleepers
BABY MANUAL

Welcome to the End of Exhaustion

Christine Scheepers

First published by Ultimate World Publishing 2022
Copyright © 2022 Christine Scheepers

ISBN

Paperback: 978-1-922714-35-0
Ebook: 978-1-922714-36-7

Christine Scheepers has asserted her rights under the Copyright, Designs and Patents Act 1988 to be identified as the author of this work. The information in this book is based on the author's experiences and opinions. The publisher specifically disclaims responsibility for any adverse consequences which may result from use of the information contained herein. Permission to use information has been sought by the author. Any breaches will be rectified in further editions of the book.

All rights reserved. No part of this publication may be reproduced, stored in or introduced into a retrieval system, or transmitted in any form, or by any means (electronic, mechanical, photocopying, recording or otherwise) without the prior written permission of the author. Any person who does any unauthorised act in relation to this publication may be liable to criminal prosecution and civil claims for damages. Enquiries should be made through the publisher.

Cover design: Ultimate World Publishing
Layout and typesetting: Ultimate World Publishing
Editor: Rebecca Low
Cover photo license is: Natalija Brenca-shuttterstock.com

Ultimate World Publishing
Diamond Creek,
Victoria Australia 3089
www.writeabook.com.au

Author's Note

I'm an ICU Registered Nurse and a midwife but the information in this book isn't medical advice. The advice you receive from me is for informational purposes only and is intended for use with common early childhood sleep issues that are wholly unrelated to medical conditions.

My advice isn't intended to be a substitute for medical advice or treatment. Always seek the advice of your doctor or other qualified health practitioners regarding any matters that may require medical attention or diagnosis, and before following the advice and using the techniques described in the Happy Sleepers Program. Reliance on any information provided by this book is solely at your own risk.

Exclusion/Limitation of Liability: In no event will Christine Scheepers from Happy Sleepers be liable to you for any claim, losses, or damages.

Thank you

For simplicity in this book, I have used "mums" when referring to parents (mum & dad) and "he" when referring to a baby and I named him Michael. Please read this book by adapting it as necessary to your situation. I'm aware of different family structures and the challenges unique to each.

Love Notes

Parents of newborns:

Sibel Remzi
EXTREMELY HAPPY! Didn't think it was possible to sleep train a ten-week-old but it definitely changed our lives! I couldn't be happier. Thank you, Christine! :)

Linda Giampa
Best investment for our little one thus far!

Being a first-time mum during stage 4 Covid restrictions has been extremely challenging. But what had presented in our little one from 4 weeks old had me question my mothering skills.

Colic was getting the better of our little one. She was not sleeping well (day and night) and when she did, she would be catnapping on my chest (and only my chest).

I decided to reach out to Christine when Bubs was 10 weeks old as we could no longer function. The little things like showering, going to the toilet, eating, and sleeping (of course) became very challenging as I was not able to put our little one down or have my husband hold her. Admittedly, I was very sceptical after hearing how sleeping training only lasts for a little while but after reading all the reviews, I sensed this could be it.

From the third night, our little one was self-settling and fast asleep within 5 to 10 minutes! I couldn't believe it and now we've a much happier Bubs as she's getting the right amount of quality sleep! It gets better, she sleeps through some nights or otherwise wakes once for a feed. This is a huge difference going from 3 to 5 feeds a night before training.

We can't thank Christine enough for the support, especially on night 1! You've been a lifesaver and we're all sleeping now.

Thank you, thank you, thank you! 😊😊

Parents of 4-month-olds to 2.5-year-olds

Alex Henderson
We can't highly recommend this program enough!

The first night starting the program was tough but with Christine's help, our 8-month-old has gone from waking several times a night crying, to sleeping through the night for 11 to 12 hours unassisted. Our son is so much more settled and happy after getting a good night's sleep (and so are his parents)!

Lana Boutos
This program has changed our lives. My 6-month-old son Dimitri was waking up every 2 hours at night and only catnapping during the day. After just a few nights, we got rid of the dummy and noticed a complete change. Now, my boy is sleeping through from 7 pm until 6:30 am! I would recommend Christine to everyone, our family is so much happier! :)

Linda Zeine
Christine did such an amazing job. My 5-month-old would only sleep with my assistance and wouldn't stay asleep unless I resettled him. However, through the help of Christine, he now falls asleep on his own and stays asleep. No dummy, no rocking, no patting and no pacing. I have my sanity back!! He's a whole new baby. He's not so clingy or grumpy during the day anymore because he's now a happy sleeper! I can't recommend her enough. THANK YOU CHRISTINE!

Parents of 3-year-olds and older

Nafiya Nadeem
People who think there are no angels on earth should speak to Christine! With her help, we're able to get our 3.5-year-old son to sleep through the night!! He hardly slept through the night before that, and his sleep time and naps were all over the place. Her guidance and sleep program have changed my toddler's life. He isn't cranky during the daytime and

doesn't take a nap anymore at day-care. We're forever in debt to Christine and would recommend her to anyone with a child having sleep issues in a heartbeat!!

Jess Mayk

I would highly recommend Happy Sleepers to everyone. Christine was amazing and her program worked!!

My nearly 4-year-old daughter was a shocking sleeper. It sometimes took hours for her to go to sleep, constantly waking up during the night and more often than not, she ended up in our bed when we're too exhausted to take her back to her bed for the 15th time that night.

She now settles herself quickly to sleep and wakes after 12 hours of rest. She has grown up so much, her behaviour is better and she's a much happier little lady (and so are we).

Thank you, Christine!!

Reem

The best thing we've done and we can't thank CHRISTINE enough 😊😊😊😊😊😊💕💕💕💕

Bianca

My husband and I still can't believe our daughter now sleeps through the night! We're so grateful we got Christine out and had her support throughout the entire program.

I never felt alone or like giving up as the program proved to me it does work. To watch my daughter learn over those weeks to put herself to sleep and to re-settle on her own was one of the most rewarding things I've ever done as a mother. Most of all, I never felt guilty or bad because the first 9 days I was with her.

I now feel well-rested, happier and more in control of our lives. My daughter is a much better eater, drinker and happier girl from getting a solid night's sleep. Thank you so much, Christine. You truly are a blessing.

Samer
At first, we're sceptical about going ahead with sleep training but decided to bite the bullet with Christine. No doubt the first night was tough with bub balling her eyes out for an hour or so but ended up sleeping through the whole night on the first night and got better day by day. We went from a restless baby and baby that had to be carried to fall asleep to a baby that napped 3 times a day and slept through the night by herself. Amazing!

Kerry
We worked with Christine when our little one was 4 months old and we had absolutely got to our wits end. Christine was calm but assertive, just what we needed and her support throughout the program was invaluable. We now have a happy little lady who's definitely getting enough quality sleep and we couldn't have done it without the help of Christine.

Vanissa
Our decision to sleep train our child at 14 months was life-changing. I used to co-sleep with my child who would wake up

3-5 times a night to feed. It was taking a toll on me, mentally and physically. Then, our friend who is based in Melbourne (we're in Queensland) recommended Happy Sleepers. Christine was very professional and supportive from day 1. Now hubby, myself and our child can get our sleep through the night, and our child is a lot happier and more engaged at kindy. I highly recommend Christine. Thanks, Christine!

Jared

Christine has been absolutely amazing! My wife and I struggled big-time with the day naps for our daughter Amelia. We couldn't work out a routine either and really needed help. Happy Sleepers came highly recommended by our neighbours and we booked in Christine ASAP.

Since we started, we haven't looked back—Amelia is happier and sleeps 3-5 hours a day and now also sleeps through the night.

We highly recommend Christine's approach—it's gentle but firm and we're so happy we decided to proceed with her.

Peter

Christine and her program were a tremendous help to us and our little girl. She was responsive and has continued being so with us even after our 14-day package, which is most appreciated particularly being first-time parents! We highly recommend Christine, her knowledge is phenomenal and we've seen fantastic results.

Eliza

Christine's program saw my 2-year-old going from waking 14 times a night to now sleeping through! I definitely recommend this program to everyone with a small child that isn't sleeping! From birth onwards!!

Jess (Angus) 2y
Guess who slept 7:15 to 7:00 no whining??

"I feel human again"

"We now have a stable routine allowing my husband, son, and I the rest we need which has brought harmony to our household."

"Thank you for giving our family back their sanity"

"It has truly changed my whole experience of being a first time mother"

Happy?!? I'm over the moon- your structured plan has given me the confidence to trust that he can do it all on his own and all he needs is my support. I'm loving this knowledge that I never had it's been great.

Morning Christine, I couldn't wait to share the good news with you. Lori finally can comfort herself to sleep during the night. She woke up 3times last night (10pm, 1am, 5am) and after crying for 6-10mins, she laid down and went back to sleep.

"I feel our lives have changed for the better - just when I had almost given up all hope."

"It definitely changed our lives!"

Happy Sleepers - Baby & Toddler Sleep Specialist & Therapist
Website Save Call
5.0 ★★★★★ 134 Google reviews

"NOW WE HAVE A GREAT ROUTINE AND TIME SPEND TOGETHER"

Acknowledgements

I want to thank my entire family, but especially my husband Carel, who offered me extraordinary support, endless encouragement and a willing ear, even when they were tired of hearing about sleep.

A special thank you to my twins, Anthony and Emma who were my first clients. Mummy loves you so much!

I also would like to thank each and every family who trusted me with their baby or toddler's sleep, even in the difficult days. We laughed together, cried, shared our frustrations but we also celebrated huge progress and successes. Thank you for letting me into your lives and for allowing me to learn along with you.

Without ALL of you, this book and Happy Sleepers would never have been possible.

- Christine Scheepers

Contents

Introduction:
Who am I?	17
A Very Important Note	21
Does This Sound Familiar?	25

Part 1: Building up your knowledge:
Building Up Your Knowledge	27
Why Is Sleep Important?	29
How Much Sleep Does a Baby Need?	37
Why Is My Baby Unable to Self-Settle?	38
Do I Have to Sleep Train My Baby?	40
Is My Baby Too Young?	41
I Am So Scared of the Crying	42
Why Does My Baby Wake Up as Soon as I Put Him Down in the Cot?	59
Why Are Structure and Routine Helpful?	63

Part 2: Let's get prepared:

Let's Get Prepared	67
The Nursery	69
Milk Feed and Solids	77
Sleeping Bags and Swaddles	85
Screen Time	90
Teething	91
Tired Signs	94
Awake Time	95
Sleep Associations	101
Pickups	109
Twins	111

Part 3: Action:

Newborn (0 to 4.5 months) — 117

- Introduction 117
- Awake time 119
- Daytime routine 120
- Bedtime routine 122
- Bedtime 124
- Overnight waking and feeding 126
- Nap routine 128
- Nap 129
- Nap emergency 130
- Short naps 133
- Summary 134

Infants (4.5 months to 7 months) — 138

- Introduction 138
- Awake time 140
- Daytime routine 140

Contents

- Bedtime 142
- Overnight waking and feeding 143
- Nap routine 146
- Nap 146
- Nap emergency 148
- Short naps 150
- Summary 151

Infants (7 months to 13 months)   155

- Introduction 155
- Awake time 156
- Daytime routine 156
- Bedtime 158
- Overnight waking and feeding 160
- Nap routine 162
- Nap 162
- Nap emergency 163
- Short naps 165
- Summary 167

Infants (13 months to 19 months) - Cot   170

- Introduction 170
- Awake time 171
- Daytime routine 171
- Bedtime 173
- Overnight waking (no feeding) 174
- Nap routine 176
- Nap 176
- Nap emergency 177
- Short naps 178
- Summary 180

Toddlers (19 months to 4 years) - Cot   183
- Introduction 183
- Awake time 184
- Daytime routine 185
- Bedtime routine 186
- Bedtime 187
- Overnight waking 190
- Nap routine 192
- Nap 193
- Nap emergency 194
- Short naps 195
- Summary 196

Toddlers in a bed (>2.5 years – In a toddler bed) 200
- Introduction 200
- Consequences, rewards, and constant requests 201
- Awake time 205
- Daytime routine 205
- Bedtime 207
- Overnight waking 208
- Nap routine 210
- Nap 211
- Nap emergency 212
- Short naps 212
- Summary 214

Part 4: Maintain

General Questions and Troubleshooting   217
How do I go on holiday? 219
Travelling by car/flying 221
I want to visit friends and go to a restaurant .. 222

Contents

- My baby is sick, what do I do? 223
- I don't want to stay at home all the time 223
- Early morning wake-ups 223
- Day-care 224
- When do I move my toddler from a cot to a toddler bed? 225
- How to keep my 2- to 2.5-year-old in the cot? 226
- When and how to move from 3 naps to 2? 228
- When and how to move from 2 naps to 1? 228
- When and how to move from 1 nap to none? 229
- Milestones to look out for 230
- Constipation 234
- Reflux 237
- Is it normal for my baby to be so clingy? 238
- My baby cries as soon as I put him down on the changing table to change his nappy, is that normal? 238
- My baby is still tired when I wake him from his last nap, can I let him sleep longer? 238
- Do I have to wake my baby up at 7:00 am or can I let him sleep in? 238
- My baby wakes up multiple times overnight, cries for a few minutes, and then goes back to sleep, is that normal? 238
- My baby takes 20 to 30 minutes to go to sleep, why is that? 239
- If I gave Nurofen/Panadol at bedtime, do I have to give it again overnight? 239
- I have already given Nurofen for 3 days, shouldn't I stop it? 239
- Will the crying harm my baby or break the bond between us? 239
- Will my baby still love me? 240

Introduction

Who am I?

Firstly, I would like to congratulate you for making this first step towards improving your baby or toddler's sleep. Just know you're not alone. There are so many parents out there who are frustrated and overwhelmed. I know you're exhausted, and I also understand that all you want is what is best for your baby. You know something needs to change, but it can be difficult to know what to do. Maybe you've read a book or two on sleep or asked around to get advice, but now you're just feeling overwhelmed (and more exhausted)! There is so much information out there and you just don't know what to follow and what to ignore. So, I just want to say, well done for making the first step towards good sleeping. A lot of parents feel, if they ask for help, they've failed as a parent because, really, "How difficult can it be to get a baby to sleep?" I can reassure you, it can be very challenging!! I hear this all the time: **"Babies don't come with a manual." Well, that's why I'm here…I'm writing the manual for you!** ☺

Babies don't come with a manual! How are you supposed to know what is the right thing and the wrong thing to do?

But first, let me introduce myself to you. My name is Christine, also known as the "Sleep fairy" or the "Baby Whisperer" or the "Sleep Lady". I will tell you a little bit about myself, and where my business comes from, so you feel a bit more comfortable and know that I do have the qualifications and experience to work with your baby and change your life forever ☺.

I'm originally from South Africa. We left South Africa in 2005, travelled to the UK and spent about 2 years there. In 2007, we moved to Australia, and Australia became our new forever home. I have worked at The Alfred Hospital as an ICU nurse since 2007 and loved it. We started our very emotional IVF journey in 2008 and were blessed with twins in 2012. Emma and Anthony were, for obvious reasons, VERY precious to us. I was a very anxious mum and never wanted them to cry for even a second. I ALWAYS responded to them immediately, even when they really didn't need me. Because of that, I just became more and more exhausted and by the time they were 4 months old, I was soooooooo tired and ready to kill everyone around me (not really ☺).

We seriously needed help. We went to sleep school but unfortunately for us, it didn't work. I did my research, and I

Who am I?

found an online DIY program. Within 7 days, both my babies were sleeping through the night and I thought, "Wow, this is amazing!!!" I felt like a new person. Had time for myself, I had time for my husband, we were all rested again, and we were able to enjoy our babies the way we wanted to. It was soooo good.

When they were not sleeping, we realised how important sleep is and how the lack of it made us a dysfunctional family. It really became my mission to help other parents with their babies' and toddlers' sleep challenges. In 2015, I underwent a comprehensive training and mentoring program in the US. It gave me the tools and knowledge to help parents with their sleep challenges and to turn sleep issues into healthy sleep habits. I started Happy Sleepers in June 2015 and since then, Happy Sleepers has helped more than 1500 parents. We have a very proud 98% success rate!! ☺

Studies have shown, UNRESOLVED sleep issues during Infancy (0 – 12 months) can persist in 80% of children until they're 3 years old!!! ☹

A Very Important Note

EVERYONE needs sleep, whether you're a baby, a teenager, or an adult. It's a basic, universal, human need and just because you decided to have a family, it does not mean you must give up your sleep. It doesn't mean you have to give up your relationship, it doesn't mean you have to give up your career/business and it certainly doesn't mean that you, as a parent, don't matter anymore. I feel very strongly about this. Yes, adults must be a bit more adaptable and cope with a bit more broken sleep in the initial stages when your baby is a newborn, but it doesn't mean you just have to accept that you'll not get your sleep or your life back because you have a baby now. It isn't fair on ANY parent.

Mums can be brutal, especially in mothers groups and in mums Facebook groups. I have seen so many mums who ask for help in one of the following ways:

- "My baby sleeps on top of me the whole day, I can't take it anymore."
- "My baby doesn't sleep at all during the day, I can't get anything done."
- "I have to lay down with my baby every single nap and bedtime otherwise he will not sleep."
- "I don't spend any time with my partner/husband anymore."

And then they get the following advice:

- "Your baby will grow out of it, just be patient."
- "You chose to be a parent."
- "Enjoy the cuddles, they're only small for a short time."
- "You'll miss it when it's gone."
- "You'll be fine."

We all need sleep, parents too!

What kind of advice is that?? Mummy guilt is already a big problem but to make a mum feel guilty because she wants to solve a problem which is affecting her mental health, is in my opinion, UNACCEPTABLE! Is a mum's life worth nothing once she had a baby? Is a mum not allowed to sleep anymore? Is a mum not allowed to sit down on the couch and have a break? Is a mum not allowed to put her baby down and do something for herself? Is a mum not allowed to spend alone time with her partner/husband?

As a twin mum, I always felt guilty when I was cuddling one baby and not the other one at the same time. I felt guilty

A Very Important Note

when I stopped breastfeeding. I felt guilty when I started thinking of sleep training and then I felt even worse when I started implementing it and someone said to me: "You're the worst mother." ☹

I get so upset when I talk about this topic because I see so many relationships break down because their baby isn't sleeping. Sleep plays a role in EVERY ASPECT OF LIFE! If your baby isn't sleeping and it's starting to affect your sleep, your mental health, or your relationship, do something about it TODAY! Don't allow any person (another mum, family, friends) to make you feel guilty about taking action. You are VERY IMPORTANT too, not only your child. If you're mentally, physically, and emotionally exhausted, how on earth are you going to be able to parent properly? Self-care is very important.

Does This Sound Familiar?

Do any of these **sound** familiar?

- Your child will only fall asleep while feeding.
- Your child needs a dummy to fall asleep.
- You're waking up with your child one, two, three (or more) times each night.
- Your child needs to be rocked, bounced, or patted in order to fall asleep.
- Your own lack of sleep is starting to take a toll on you and your family.

Do any of these **feel** familiar?

- I'm exhausted all the time.
- I don't enjoy having others around me.
- I don't enjoy being a mother anymore.
- I feel like a failure.
- I'm not a good mother to my child/children.

Happy Sleepers

I was in a bad space with no sleep and I had no idea what to do! I spent 9 months on two to three hours of sleep a night and no rest during the day.

- Mary

I felt like this ALL the time when my twins were babies and ALL my ex-clients felt the same too, **BUT**...do you know what the great news is...

It can all change TODAY!
Starting right here, right NOW!!!

Do you want to be part of our success story?

Part 1:

Building Up Your Knowledge

Why Is Sleep Important?

In many households, one parent must go off to work early every morning, which can make night-time waking a real bone of contention. On the one hand, mum or dad really do need sleep to deal with the demands of a day at the office, but it's also important for the other parent to get his or her sleep as well. After all, a day with children is awfully demanding too!

Most of the families I work with, the mother ends up fighting most of the night time battles all by herself. Unfortunately, this can often lead to feelings of resentment towards her partner, or even toward her child.

A study in the June 2001 issue of Pediatrics related infant sleep problems to postnatal depression, showed that mothers of poor sleepers, consistently have more depressive symptoms than mothers of good sleepers. This makes perfect sense; anyone's mood is bound to turn sour after several days—or weeks, or even months—of continued sleep deprivation. This lack of sleep can cause parents to become obsessed with the idea of sleep. I remember meeting with a mother named Wendy who told me an interesting story:

"I remember looking at other women on the streets or in grocery stores and instead of thinking, 'Oh, I wish I had hair like hers,' or 'What a great figure she has,' I started thinking, 'Look how well-rested she looks…I bet she sleeps through the night!' Whenever I would meet with other mothers and discover that their children had always slept through the night, I would be very envious. They would try to offer helpful hints, or say things like, 'They'll grow out of it,' but I was really beginning to doubt that he ever would!"

The frustration of not getting enough sleep is by no means limited to mothers, a father at one of my seminars began the day by declaring that his daughter was the first and only child he was ever going to have. It was just too hard on both him and his wife to be getting up every 2 hours during the night. He felt his wife was taking out all her frustrations on him, and it was causing too much strain on their relationship. He swore that if things didn't change quickly and dramatically, he was going to have a vasectomy! Thankfully, his daughter's sleep issues were soon under control, and he and his wife are now planning to have another baby very soon.

> Sleep is the power source that keeps your mind alert and calm. Every night and at every nap, sleep recharges the brain's battery.

Why Is Sleep Important?

Of course, if you're reading this book, you most likely already know how terrible it feels to not get enough sleep. So, let's move on to a brief discussion of why your child may be having difficulty sleeping.

How important is sleep?

> "Sleep is the power source that keeps your mind alert and calm. Every night and at every nap, sleep recharges the brain's battery. Sleeping well, increases brainpower just as weightlifting builds stronger muscles because sleeping well increases your attention span and allows you to be physically relaxed and mentally alert at the same time. Then you're at your personal best."
> **– Dr. Marc Weissbluth, author of Healthy Sleep Habits, Happy Child**

When I'm explaining the importance of sleep to my clients during a seminar, I like to make a comparison between sleeping and eating. Both are necessary for survival. When people eat an unhealthy diet, they become malnourished, and their body suffers in the same way, people who have unhealthy sleep habits become mentally malnourished. Lack of sleep starves them of the energy they need to be happy and well adjusted.

No sane parents would raise their children entirely on a diet of candy, because everyone knows that it wouldn't only be terribly unhealthy for their children but would also teach them bad eating habits—habits they would carry with them throughout their childhood and probably for the rest of their lives. Unfortunately, our society isn't nearly as well-educated about the importance of sleep as we are about the importance of eating a balanced and nutritious diet.

The good news is that doctors and the rest of the medical community have become more vocal about the importance of a healthy night's sleep in the past few years. Dr. William Dement, the founder of the Stanford University Sleep Research Centre, has conducted extensive research that suggests sleep is the single most important factor in predicting how long people will live—more influential than diet, exercise, or heredity.

Our society is especially ignorant of the importance of sleep for infants and toddlers. Current research shows that between 20 and 30 percent of all infants and toddlers will have some difficulty sleeping but many parents tell themselves, "They'll grow out of it," the truth is that most of these cases persist for 3 to 5 years.

Sleep plays a role in every aspect of life!

Infants or toddlers who aren't getting enough sleep are easy to spot. They'll frequently rub their eyes and faces throughout the day, and they're more likely to suddenly "lose it." We've all had experiences where our child starts throwing a tantrum in public; these breakdowns are far more common for children who are tired than for those who have been getting the sleep they need.

Why Is Sleep Important?

Many sleep-deprived children also start to develop behaviours that are usually called "overactive" or "hyperactive." They may even be labelled as "attention-deficit" children. Dr. Judith Owens, the director of the Paediatric Sleep Disorders Clinic and the Learning, Attention, and Behaviour Program at Hasbro Children's Hospital in Providence, Rhode Island, notes that there is a huge overlap between sleep deprivation and psychiatric disorders such as attention-deficit/hyperactivity disorder.

The bottom line is this: Sleep is tremendously important. It's just as important for your child as a healthy diet or a loving home. If your child isn't getting enough sleep every day, he's being put at a disadvantage. He'll not be able to deal with the pressures of the day as well as his peers, and he'll probably have a more difficult time acquiring and retaining knowledge than a child who is getting the proper amount of sleep.

The importance of the "right kind" of sleep

Sleep experts agree that "consolidated" (uninterrupted) sleep is the most restful and healthy kind of sleep for both infants and adults. Sleep that's interrupted by one or more awakenings during the night usually leads to daytime sleepiness, a decrease in mental flexibility and attention, and mood impairments. In other words, sleep that's broken up by several "night wakings" isn't the same as sleeping through the night. So, it's important that adults and children get all the consolidated sleep they need. Even adults who have had just one night of fragmented sleep show a dramatic reduction in motivation and attention. They often feel overwhelmed by the tasks of the day and have difficulty making decisions. The effects on infants and children are even more harmful.

For both adults and children to function at their peak performance, they must be getting adequate, consolidated sleep. Children who sleep 10 to 12 hours a night wake up well-rested, attentive, cheerful, and are best able to cope with and learn from their environment. Parents, too, will feel better equipped to perform the demanding tasks of work and family life. Sleep is important for you too!

I hope you're starting to see how incredibly important sleep is for your child. Once you've implemented the system in this book and your little one is consistently sleeping through the night, I think you'll be amazed at how much happier and more alert he'll be during the day. But it's just as important that you understand how important sleep is for you and your partner as well! Sleep deprivation is a powerful thing, and if you've noticed a negative change in yourself and your spouse since your child arrived (or since his sleep difficulties began), there's a good chance that this change has been caused by the fact that you're simply not getting enough sleep.

For many new parents, the first few months of parenthood, are the first time in their lives they are prevented from getting as much sleep as they want. Gone are the days of lazing around in bed until 11:00 on a Saturday morning—because your new baby is now waking you up at 5:00 am! And as if that weren't bad enough, you're also getting up a number of times every night to feed or rock your child back to sleep.

Why Is Sleep Important?

Now, if this is your first child and he is less than a few months old, you might not notice the effects of this sleep deprivation. After all, you've this wonderful new person to care for, and nothing else seems to matter very much. But believe me, after a few more months of not getting enough sleep, not even the joy of being a new parent will replace your need for a decent night's sleep!

The National Sleep Foundation recently released a comprehensive study showing that parents of children with sleep difficulties get an average of 6.8 hours of sleep per night—considerably less than the 8 hours adults typically need to feel rested and function optimally. When we're tired, we're cranky and when we're cranky, we tend to take it out on those closest to us. For most families, this means that your spouse is the one who receives the brunt of your grouchiness. The job of raising children is tough at times, and you need to be able to count on the love and support of your partner. That support can be hard to muster up at times if you're always at each other's throats because you're both so darn tired all the time!

In addition, tired parents are likely to suffer at work. Of course, employers are usually pretty forgiving of the forgetfulness and fatigue new parents experience during the first few months of their child's life, but if you've been showing up for work utterly exhausted for the past year, then you can be pretty sure that the quality of your work has been suffering.

Problems with your spouse or poor work performance has frightening possible outcomes. However, the most serious consequence of sleep deprivation is that it can lead to dangerous feelings of disappointment, resentment, or even anger toward your child. Early childhood is when we learn a great deal about emotions, so if you're often grouchy with your child, your behaviour can have a strong negative impact on how your child interacts with others as he gets older.

Some of my clients have privately confessed to being so fed up with their child's crying in the middle of the night that they've occasionally had thoughts about shaking their baby. Of course, they've never done it. But the thought itself can be terrifying for parents and I'm sure that for every parent who has told me about these feelings, there are a dozen more who feel the same way but are too embarrassed to tell me.

So, sleep is undeniably important—not just for your child, but for you and the rest of your family as well. If you have children who are already in school and are being awakened in the night by a crying baby, it can have a terrible effect on their emotional health and, of course, their schoolwork.

The good news is that there is an easy solution to all these problems. Once your child is sleeping through the night, most of these problems will start to melt away. You and your spouse will be able to start spending some quality time together again…You'll feel ready to face the day when you wake up in the morning…Your friends and co-workers will start to notice a real change in your mood and the way you look.

Sounds good? Then let us get started!

How Much Sleep Does a Baby Need?

Babies and toddlers need a lot more sleep than parents think. If a baby wakes up tired in the morning, seems cranky during the day, or tends to "lose it" sometimes in the late afternoon, your baby is probably not getting enough sleep in a 24-hour period.

Let's have a look at how much sleep your baby needs:

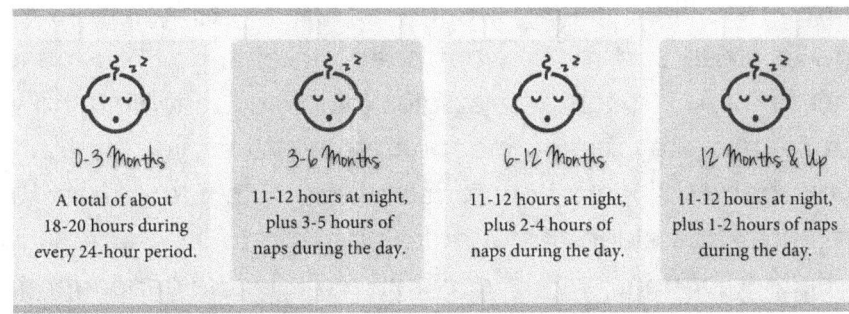

0-3 Months	3-6 Months	6-12 Months	12 Months & Up
A total of about 18-20 hours during every 24-hour period.	11-12 hours at night, plus 3-5 hours of naps during the day.	11-12 hours at night, plus 2-4 hours of naps during the day.	11-12 hours at night, plus 1-2 hours of naps during the day.

Why Is My Baby Unable to Self-Settle?

When you want to teach a baby how to self-settle, you must teach your baby proper sleep skills. You must teach him how to fall asleep INDEPENDENTLY and stay asleep INDEPENDENTLY. When anyone (baby, toddler, or adult) has the ability to do that, that person has an INTERNALISED SKILL to sleep. Like you do. You can just lie down (awake) and sleep. You don't need anyone to pat your back, rock you, put a dummy in your mouth or feed you, to sleep, but your baby can't. He needs EXTERNAL strategies like rocking, patting, or feeding to **help** him to go to sleep and that's what needs to change. You must get rid of ALL external strategies (help) and teach him how to fall and stay asleep independently. When you do that, your baby will learn how to fall asleep within less than 10 minutes and sleep through the night (11 to 12 hours with one feed or none) within less than a week (age dependent).

Why Is My Baby Unable to Self-Settle?

Everyone (adults and children alike) wakes up several times each night – but for most of us, those awakenings are so brief that we don't even remember them in the morning (when your child is slept trained ☺)

Do I Have to Sleep Train My Baby?

If you're happy with the sleep situation you're in at the moment, and everyone who lives in the house feels well-rested in the morning then no, you don't have to sleep train your baby, but if someone isn't getting enough rest overnight because your baby needs you multiple times to help him go back to sleep, it's a problem. Yes, babies who are 6 months and younger might need a feed once or twice overnight but in between, he must have a solid sleep and not need you to help him go back to sleep every time he wakes up.

Is My Baby Too Young?

You don't have to sleep train a young baby (newborn) but establishing good sleeping habits, structure and routine will help them to start sleeping well as soon as possible.

I Am So Scared of the Crying

The single biggest issue I encounter as a baby/toddler sleep specialist is the question of crying. Is it okay to let your child "cry it out"? If so, how much crying should you put up with? How long will a baby cry before he falls asleep? Is it healthy? Won't your baby resent you if you just let him cry all by himself?

Now, before you start to worry that I'm an advocate of the "cry it out" school of sleep training, please don't panic! I'm not. So please keep reading…

I remember when my husband and I finally decided that we've had enough of the sleepless nights and started the process of teaching our little twins to sleep through the night. The idea of listening to them crying alone—for who knows how long— was terrifying. In fact, it was this fear that had prevented us from taking this step on several previous occasions.

I Am So Scared of the Crying

To combat our fear, we decided to take a good hard look at our situation. As a couple, we had begun to feel the strains of all our sleepless nights. We were staying up until midnight, only getting a few hours of uninterrupted sleep at a time, having very little time alone, and not connecting the same way we used to. We could see that if things continued this way much longer, we would begin to drift apart, and our relationship would pay the price. That was something we refused to let happen.

We looked at how we were functioning as parents. I was tired, worried, depressed, and feeling resentment toward my husband—and even worse, my babies! Since neither my husband nor I had enjoyed a decent night's sleep in months, we're both grouchy a lot of the time. We decided to make a list of the pros and cons involved in teaching our twins to sleep through the night. On the "pros" side, we would no longer have any of the problems I just described, and—much more importantly—our twins would be happier and healthier because sleep is so important for the emotional and physical wellbeing of infants and toddlers.

We also knew that our families, friends, and parents would be greatly relieved to know that we would finally be getting some sleep and have the energy to spend some quality time with them, instead of turning down their invitations to dinners, parties, and all the other get-togethers that we're always too tired to attend.

The list was getting long on the "pros" side, so we decided to move on to the "cons". We were only able to come up with one reason why we didn't want to go ahead with teaching our twins how to sleep through the night. That one reason was that they were going to cry. The very idea of letting them cry had been enough to hold us back from even trying to teach them to sleep through the night. As we sat there and looked at our long list of pros, and then looked at the only thing we were able to identify as a con, we knew that we had made our decision.

Looking back, there was not much to be afraid of. We did have to put up with a bit of crying for the first night or 2, but it was manageable because we knew there was a purpose, and the end result was that everyone—especially our twins—was actually much happier now that we're all getting some sleep.

As hard as it is to listen to your child cry, it's important to remember that infants and toddlers only have a couple of ways to communicate with us. When they're pleased, they smile, coo, giggle, and laugh. When they're angry, upset, hungry, uncomfortable, irritated, frustrated, tired, or grouchy, they cry.

Now, just as the smallest things can cause your little one to start laughing hysterically, so too can any minor annoyance launch him into a fit of crying. Have you ever let your 8-month-old play with a set of your keys, and then had to take them away because you needed to get the car started and drive somewhere? Many children will cry their lungs out if we take something away from them! But if you happen to need whatever it is they're playing with, or if they're playing with

I Am So Scared of the Crying

something dangerous, you have no choice in the matter. You have to act in their best interest, even if it results in tears.

> Crying doesn't always mean something is wrong, your child may be irritated, frustrated, tired, or grouchy.

One day, my daughter had her own juice cup and the juice cup of another toddler in her hands and was happily running around with both. It wasn't until the owner of the second juice cup came over to ask for his cup back that the problem began. Emma absolutely didn't want to give back the boy's cup. Of course, I tried to reason with her, explaining that she really didn't need 2 juice cups and that one did, in fact, belong to the other child, but nothing would convince her.

When I finally had to take the cup from Emma, she had a complete meltdown. She cried, kicked, and threw herself around on the floor for at least 15 minutes. Finally, I scooped her up, struggled to get her into the car, and took her home. She cried madly for most of the ride home as well. Needless to say, it was a terrible ordeal for both of us. I was almost in tears just watching her, but I realised there was truly nothing I could do to help her. I could make sure she was safe and be there waiting with open arms when she stopped crying, but for as long as the tantrum lasted, I knew there was nothing I could do.

Now, if my daughter was a bit older and knew how to talk, I would have been able to reason with her, and she would have been able to explain to me why she was so upset and what she would like me to do, to make it better. Unfortunately, infants and toddlers can't hold rational conversations with us, so they communicate with us the only way they know how. They laugh and smile when they're happy, and they cry when they're upset.

It *doesn't get* easier as they get older.

I often meet with parents of 2 and 3-year-olds who are still waking up a couple of times every night and help them fall back asleep (either by getting them a bottle of milk, holding their hands, or taking their child to bed with them). When I ask these parents why on earth, they've waited so long to call me, they almost always give me the same answer: "We thought he would grow out of it."

The bad news is children usually don't grow out of it. Current research shows that infants who are having sleep difficulties, continue to do so for 3 to 5 years. I can certainly vouch for this. At least half of the clients I have worked with over the years have had children over the age of 2, so the idea that babies will grow out of it as they get older simply isn't usually true. Unfortunately, as your child gets older, it also gets harder, not easier, to see them cry. As a daughter, I can tell you that it still breaks my mother's heart to see me cry. It's something that never gets easier to bear. All parents hold their child's happiness foremost in their minds. It doesn't matter how old your child is, you're simply never going to enjoy seeing them upset. The one thing that's critical for parents to remember is that crying isn't going to cause **any** damage to a child.

I Am So Scared of the Crying

Children cry a lot. They cry for any reason. They cry for **no** reason. Sometimes they cry just to get our attention. Crying at bedtime isn't any different than crying during the day, but for some reason, it's much harder for most parents to take.

You can't please your child all the time.

Sometimes the hardest thing to face when you're a parent is the fact that in some circumstances, the best thing you can do for your child is nothing at all. Remember the story I told you about my daughter throwing a tantrum because she couldn't have 2 cups of juice? Well, I couldn't give her back the cup, since that would be rewarding the tantrum, which would no doubt result in the same sort of situation happening over and over again. I couldn't comfort her because she didn't want me near her, and she was far too young to reason with. The only thing I could do was simply let her be. She had to work out her distress all on her own. I could be there for her when she was finished with her tantrum, and I could reassure her with my voice that everything was okay, but in the end, it was up to her to calm herself down.

It's important to remember this lesson when your child cries during the first few nights. He's learning to fall asleep on his own. Children need to realise that they have control over their own bodies. They need to learn how to recognise what "tired" feels like, and how to alleviate those tired feelings without anyone's help. It's important for them to understand that sleep isn't a scary place, a bad thing, a punishment, or a battle that must be fought, but a nice, warm, comfortable place… to put tired feelings to rest so they can wake up in the morning feeling happy, refreshed, and ready for a new day.

Once my clients have finished my program, they often tell me that their children have started to ask to go to bed. Or they'll ask for a bath and start walking to the bathroom, knowing that a bath is the first step of their bedtime routine. They'll even point to their cots and say "night-night" when they're feeling sleepy.

The first time your child exhibits this kind of behaviour will almost certainly be a very rewarding experience for you because it will be clear that your child understands the reason for sleeping. He'll recognise what "tired" feels like and will be happy to go to bed to make those tired feelings go away. He'll look forward to his "alone time" in his room when he can have a chat with his favourite stuffed animal and tell him all about his day before finally falling asleep.

> Crying isn't going to cause any damage to your child. Children cry a lot. They cry for any reason. They cry for no reason. Sometimes they cry just to get our attention. Crying at bedtime isn't any different than crying during the day, but for some reason, it's much harder for most parents to take.

Is crying a necessary step?

Do you absolutely have to let your child cry to teach him to sleep through the night? Probably.

I'm being honest with you. I would love to tell you that I have discovered a way to teach infants and toddlers to sleep through the night that involves no protest on their part, but I have not. And despite the claims of people who will try to sell you a magic blanket or CD that's supposed to put your child instantly to sleep, I don't think that such a method exists. However, as I hope you understand by now, a little crying isn't going to do any damage to your child.

The important thing to remember is that it isn't the crying that will help your little one fall asleep—it's the self-soothing strategies that he'll have an opportunity to develop in order to stop himself from crying. His crying comes from a change to the old routine. Putting your baby in his cot at night awake might be a completely new experience for him. He'll be confused and upset by this new change, and yes, he'll probably cry to express his displeasure. But remember that your child wants to stop crying as much—if not more—than you want him to. He'll cry for a while because he knows that this is the strategy that has worked for him in the past, but once he figures out that it's up to him to get himself to sleep, he'll likely figure out how to make that happen faster than you'd think!

The bottom line is, change of any kind is a difficult thing for everyone. How many times have you vowed to eat healthier, quit smoking, or exercise more? Making change happen is tough for us adults, so it's only fair to expect our children to find it difficult as well. The good news is that infants and toddlers learn faster than we do. And as you'll soon discover, they figure out how to soothe themselves into a deep and restful sleep sooner than you would imagine.

How much crying?

So just how much crying should you expect? It depends. Some children will cry for an hour or more for the first night before they fall asleep. Usually, the second night is half the time (about 30 minutes) and the third night is usually half that time (15 minutes) which just shows you how quickly babies or toddlers learn. Others will doze off after just a few minutes. Some children will get the hang of things in a couple of days. Others will take a couple of weeks.

Here is an example for you, drawn from an experience with a family I worked with:

Liz and Mark were at their wits' end by the time they gave me a call. Their little 8-month-old boy, Lachy, had never slept for more than 2 hours at a time. When Lachy was 2 weeks old, his weight gain began to slow down. On the instruction of her doctor, Liz began to wake Lachy up every 2 hours through the night to increase his milk intake and to ensure he was getting the calories he needed. This started a terrible cycle for both Liz and Lachy because Lachy became used to waking up every 2 hours for a feed and Liz had to get up with him each time and feed him back to sleep.

I Am So Scared of the Crying

When Liz called me, she was in an awful state of mind. Lachy's weight gain was back on track, so he didn't really need to be fed every 2 hours, but it had become a habit. As a result, Liz was so sleep-deprived that her marriage was starting to suffer, she had been taking out all her frustrations on her husband.

When I met Mark, he was convinced that Lachy was going to be their only child if things continued the way they were going. He also felt that his relationship with Liz was going to be in serious trouble if things didn't change soon.

After I met with Liz and Mark and gave them all the same information I'm giving you here, they decided to give my plan a try. Liz was positive that Lachy would cry hysterically all night long if she didn't feed him, but she decided that she would at least see how long she could hold out before caving into his cries.

When I spoke to Liz the next morning, she was ecstatic! She said that they had followed their plan and had Lachy in bed by 7:00 pm. He was definitely confused by the change of events in his bedtime routine, but Liz followed her plan and after 55 minutes, Lachy was asleep. Liz, who was utterly exhausted from months of sleep deprivation, soon went to bed herself, not sure what the rest of the night had in store for her. You can imagine her surprise when she woke with a start at 1:00 am and realised that she had been asleep for almost 5 straight hours! She was convinced that something must have happened to Lachy and ran into his bedroom—only to find the little guy happily snoozing away. A few minutes later, Lachy woke up and started to cry, but Liz decided to leave him for a few minutes to see if he would go back to sleep on his own. To her surprise, he was asleep again in 9 minutes—and slept until 4:00 am. He started crying again, she left him and within 7 minutes, he was asleep again. She had to wake him at 7:00 am!!!

Liz couldn't believe how well the night went. She knew every night might not go so well but had the motivation she needed to keep going with her sleep plan. Well, it's now 9 months later and I'm happy to report that Lachy is still doing very well. He goes to bed happily at 7:00 pm and sleeps until 6 or 7 the next morning. He's also having 2 solid naps a day, and everyone is happier and healthier now that they're all sleeping through the night!

Admittedly, this is a best-case scenario. Lachy learned self-soothing strategies very quickly and continued to do well night after night. Liz and Mark were thrilled by the results. Mark later confided in me that the changes they had made to Lachy's sleep schedule had improved the quality of their relationship and also their happiness as parents. He was no longer against having more children and was happy to have his wife back!

When people ask me how long it usually takes for a child to learn how to sleep through the night, I hate to give them an answer, as it can be discouraging for them if their child takes longer than average but it usually only takes **1 week**! It takes an average of 7 nights for babies older than 7 months to sleep through the night, and will cry for 45 to 90 minutes on the first night before falling asleep on their own. These numbers are based on my work with hundreds of families, but they're still just averages. It will happen quicker for some children and slower for others.

Is this harmful?

I'm sometimes asked by concerned parents whether I think that letting their infant or toddler cry at bedtime will lead to permanent psychological damage. The answer is most definitely **NOT**! I'm unaware of any **credible** evidence from a published medical study that mentions any link between letting a child cry at bedtime for a few nights and psychological problems later in life.

Now, I'm not for a moment suggesting that you ignore the cries of your child—especially if they sound serious. If there is any possibility that your child might be crying because he's in danger or in pain, then, of course, you need to go and help him! Even if you're uncertain whether the cries of your child are serious or not, you can still go in and check on him. Simply entering the room of your child and checking to see that he's alright isn't going to prevent him from learning how to sleep through the night.

IMPORTANT NOTE: Some parents will find that their child will seem "needier" or "clingy" during the first week or 2 they start implementing a sleep schedule. This is normal for many children, and it almost always resolves itself within a week or 2.

Don't feel guilty.

Personally, I feel that one of the biggest dangers in any relationship—including the one you have with your children—is letting guilt get the best of you. Guilt is a funny thing. Someone once said: "Guilt is like sitting in a rocking chair, it'll give you something to do, but it will never get you anywhere!" Before you give in to those feelings of guilt, take a minute to think about what you're feeling guilty about. All you're doing is teaching your child an important and healthy lesson. The ability to sleep peacefully is a gift that you're giving your child, a gift that he'll be able to use for the rest of his life.

Now, I know that I feel a little guilty when my son cries because I will not give him a second—or third or fourth—piece of my chocolate bar. Of course, not filling him with chocolate is the right thing to do, and not giving in to his whining actually makes me a better parent than if I did give him an entire chocolate bar to eat. Still, I can't help but feel a bit sad for the little guy!

So, why do we find it so easy to give into guilt?

The answer is simple: We want to please other people. We especially want to please the people we love and we aren't used to people crying in order to get what they want—especially if we're first-time parents. Can you imagine what you would do if your friends, co-workers, or family members started crying whenever they didn't get what they wanted from you?

I Am So Scared of the Crying

When our children—who we love more than anyone else on this planet—start to cry, we naturally want to do whatever it takes to stop them from crying and make them happy. The problem is, giving in to that crying often means exchanging your child's wellbeing for your own peace of mind. ("This chocolate bar may not be a healthy snack for my baby, but at least he's happy. Now I don't have to feel like a monster for making him cry with all these people around us listening to him!")

I know that everyone gives in to their child from time to time. If you've ever been stuck on a crowded airplane with a crying baby, you know that you'd do anything to get him or her to stop crying. However, if you make a habit of always doing whatever it takes to stop your child from crying, then you'll end up with a real problem. Children—especially infants and toddlers—learn by observing what happens when they perform certain behaviours. When they get what they want because of a certain behaviour (getting to breastfeed whenever they cry, for example), then you can bet they'll keep repeating that behaviour for as long as it's effective!

The ability to sleep peacefully is a gift that you're giving your child, a gift that he'll be able to use for the rest of his life.

Putting it all together

So, what are my feelings and recommendations about crying? I think that it's tremendously important that children learn to sleep well. It's important for children to understand that they have the power to resolve their own sleep needs. It's important that children learn to understand what "tired" feels like and connect that to the fact that sleep is the only way to make those tired feelings go away. It's important for your child not to have anxiety or fear around going to bed. In order for your child to learn all these important things, some crying will usually be involved.

Like I said before, change is hard work. Changing your child's sleep habits will most likely be met with some protest. The best, quickest, and most effective way to teach him how to sleep through the night is to let him figure it out on his own, and yes, this will probably involve some crying but don't worry, you'll be able to sit right next to your child, talking to him, touching him and laying him down if he stands up. You'll be able to support him while he's learning.

Of course, your child will probably still cry even though you're in the room with him. He'll still want you to pick him up, give him attention and help him to sleep, but it's important that you don't give in. You're there to give occasional reassurance with touch and comfort to your child with your voice.

Final thoughts:

My goal for this chapter is that, after reading it, you'll understand that a little crying isn't the end of the world. By letting your child cry a bit and teaching him how to soothe

I Am So Scared of the Crying

himself to sleep, you're giving him an important gift that he'll carry with him throughout his entire life.

By this point in the book, I also hope that you share my appreciation for how incredibly important sleep is, especially for infants and children. They desperately need their sleep for their minds to develop properly and so that they can start each day rested, refreshed, and ready to learn. Refusing to give them the tools they need to develop healthy sleep habits will be far more harmful to your children than a few minutes of crying.

Finally, I want you to understand the difference between the strategies I'm recommending and the idea of letting a baby "cry it out." Letting a baby "cry it out" implies that you've done nothing to prepare your child for bedtime and are just going to put him into his cot, close the bedroom door, and walk away! To me, this kind of treatment is totally unfair to your child. You need to prepare him for sleep by teaching him predictable cues that tells him bedtime is approaching, and you need to make sure he knows you're there to support him. What I recommend to my clients is a complete sleep time strategy that will probably involve some crying. Where many parents go wrong is that they decide to try the so-called "cry it out" approach and then, without learning the importance of creating a bedtime routine, they just put their children into their cots and leave them! That's why it's so important for you to take the time to read through this book and educate yourself about how sleep works and why it's so critical to your child's development. By understanding how sleep happens, and by giving your child the tools he needs to soothe himself to sleep, you can rest assured that you're doing the right thing.

Why Does My Baby Wake Up as Soon as I Put Him Down in the Cot?

Now we're going to talk about something not a lot of parents know. We as human beings aren't meant to **move** while we're asleep. As soon as we start moving, **our brain** thinks: "Ok, hang on, why is my sleeping body moving? The body is in danger." The **fight-flight** mode in our bodies kicks in, and it brings the baby **out of sleep** instead of deeper into sleep. I'm pretty sure you've experienced this before (especially with newborns). You rocked or fed your baby to sleep in your arms, you're slowly moving your baby to put him down in the cot and as soon as he touches the mattress, he wakes up!!!! ☹ It's sooooo frustrating!!! Why is this happening??? You pick him up and have to start the whole process AGAIN!

- Your baby **didn't wake** up because you moved him too quickly.
- He **didn't wake** up because he wasn't fully asleep.
- He **didn't wake** up because he doesn't like the cot.
- He **woke up** because you **moved** him while he was **DROWSY/ASLEEP**.

Newborns usually wake up straight away but some newborns and older babies usually wake up within 30 minutes to 2 hours.

If you want any chance for your baby to start sleeping for longer stretches, or even have the chance to start sleeping through the night, he **must fall asleep in the cot**. That doesn't mean putting him in the cot half asleep, or half drowsy, because that's already the first stage of sleep, it's too far. Your baby must be in the cot FULLY AWAKE and fall asleep in the cot. He must be able to look around to see where he is and fall asleep from there. This is very important.

Babies and toddlers MUST be put down FULLY AWAKE, not half drowsy, or asleep.

Babies also usually wake up crying if they fell asleep in one spot and wake up in another. They almost wake up startled. This is also the case when your baby is in the car or pram. If you want your baby to sleep in the car or the pram, it's fine, but he must **finish** the sleep in the car or pram. You can't let him fall asleep and as soon as you get home or at your destination, pick him up and put him in the cot. Most babies aren't transferable. They usually wake up and you will not be able to get them back to sleep without a lot of crying. If you want your baby to have a decent nap but he fell asleep in the car, you must finish the sleep in the car. If you're close to home and your baby is trying to fall asleep, try to keep him awake. Talk to him, sing songs or do whatever it takes, but you must keep your baby fully awake in the car. As soon as you get home or at your destination, put your baby down in his cot fully awake. If he fell asleep in the car, you have to keep on driving until he finished the nap.

If you really have to pick him up, you must know that there is a good chance that he will not be able to go back to sleep and he will be grumpy. You will have to wait out his awake time and then put him down, even if it was only a 5- or 10-minute micro nap.

Keep your baby fully awake in the car. If he fell asleep in the car, you must keep on driving until he finishes the nap.

Why Are Structure and Routine Helpful?

(Daytime routine, nap routine, bedtime routine, feeding routine, eat-play-sleep)

A structured daily routine will help your baby understand what is happening now, what is going to happen next and what is expected from him. It will be much easier to manage him.

For example:

You go to the kitchen every day at a certain time (say about noon), you get a banana out with yoghurt and toast, you get your baby's plate out with his cutlery and put him in his highchair. While you're doing that, your baby is watching you. You can tell him: "Michael, we're going to have some lunch now." He doesn't necessarily understand what you're saying, especially if he's only 5 or 6 months old, but he sees your routine in the kitchen. Your routine in the kitchen is his cue to tell him, mummy is making food, I'm going to eat now. He's preparing himself psychologically to eat. The eating process will be a lot easier.

The same goes for sleep. If you have the same routine every single day before sleep, going to sleep will be so much easier. Your baby will be tired (because he's at his maximum awake time), he'll see that you're doing the nap routine, and get ready to sleep. Putting him down and having him falling asleep will be a lot easier because, psychologically, he had time to prepare himself for sleep. If you're going to change that routine every day (today I'm patting you to sleep, the next nap I'm trying to rock you to sleep, tonight I'm going to feed you to sleep, tomorrow I'm going to push you in the pram), it's confusing. Your baby has no clue what's happening and what's expected. Yes, he'll eventually fall asleep because he's exhausted, but it's hard work and emotionally painful.

The other reason why structure and routine is helpful is to find out why your baby is unhappy at a certain time. Unfortunately, tired cries and hungry cries can sound very similar and because we as parents always think our babies are hungry, whenever they cry, we feed them. That's not always helpful because you're starting a habit that will affect your baby's sleep. Your baby might just be tired and needs to be put down or your baby might be uncomfortable with teething and only need pain relief or your baby might be wet and need a nappy change. If you have a structured routine, it will be easier to eliminate reasons why your baby is crying. If your baby is on a 4-hourly feeding schedule and it has only been

Why Are Structure and Routine Helpful?

2 hours since your baby's last feed, your baby isn't crying because he's hungry. It must be something else.

When should I start a routine?

As soon as possible. I know it can be difficult to get a newborn into a routine but the more you practice, the easier it will get. Routine will also give you a sense of sanity.

Part 2:

Let's Get Prepared

The Nursery

Cot safety

- Keep the cot clear from:
    o Curtains or blinds
    o Heaters
    o Power points
- Make sure the space above the cot is free of objects, such as mirrors and pictures which could fall onto your baby.
- Remove climbing aids (such as large toys or pillows) from the cot once your child can stand.
- Don't attach musical mobiles or video monitors to the cot.
- Make sure the mattress base is at the lowest setting before your baby can sit up.
- Make sure the mattress is a good fit with no gaps between the bars and the mattress.

Cot location and position

Deciding where your baby's cot/bassinette is going to be can be a stressful decision. According to the Sudden Infant Death Syndrome (SIDS) guidelines, your baby must sleep in your room until the age of 12 months, but I don't necessarily agree with that. Babies (especially newborns) can be very noisy sleepers. They toss and turn and make noises, waking you up all the time which isn't good for your sleep. If your baby's nursery and cot/bassinette is safe (cot safety, ideal room temperature, and you have a video monitor), I can't see why your room will necessarily be safer than your baby's nursery.

I'm a big advocate for babies to sleep in their own nurseries. First of all, as I said before, it will improve the parents' sleep because it isn't noisy. The second reason is, if your baby sleeps in your room, he can hear you and smell you. If he wakes up and needs to be resettled back to sleep (it isn't time for a feed) and he can smell and hear you, it will make it a lot more difficult for your baby to resettle and go back to sleep because he knows you're there. If you really feel uncomfortable having your baby in his own nursery, please don't position your baby right next to you, have his cot in the furthest corner (in your room) away from you.

When we do the sleep training, we recommend the "camp out/sit down" method which means you sit right next to your baby until he falls asleep but gradually move away from him towards the door. We want to teach your baby how to fall asleep without your closeness. A parent can also be a sleep association. He needs your closeness to fall asleep. When

The Nursery

we do the "camp out/sit down" method we need the cot to be in the furthest corner diagonally from the door so you can move towards the door. Please see picture.

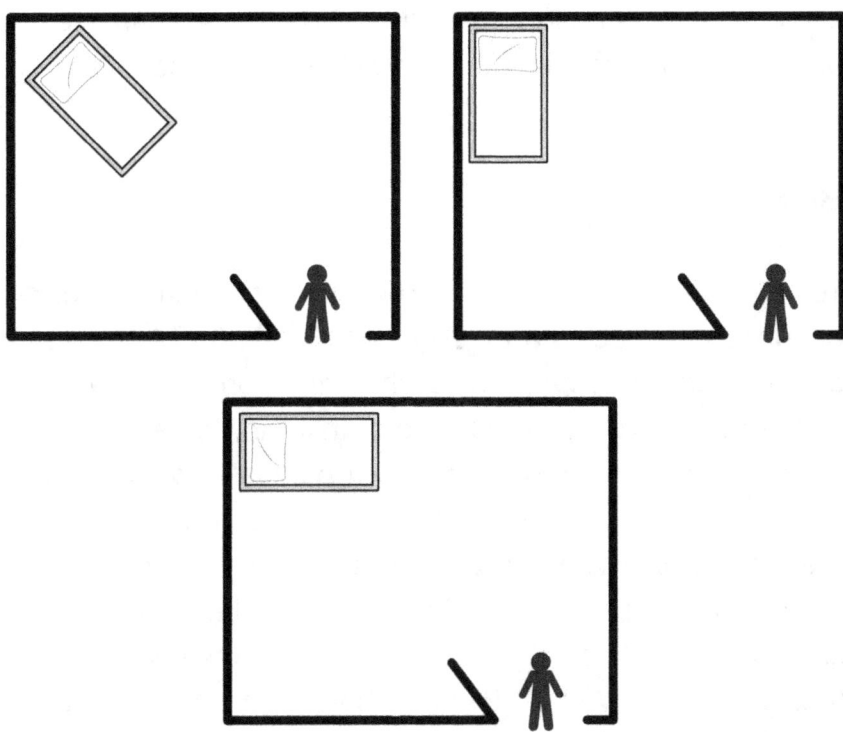

Consistency in terms of where your baby sleeps is also important. When your baby is at home (I'm not talking about when you're out or when your baby is at day-care) your baby must always sleep in the same room in the same cot (obviously if possible) . When you're at home, try not to have his naps in one room and his bedtime or overnight sleep in a different room. Again, to make it easier for your baby to know what is going on now and what is happening next. Consistency is very important.

Pillows

Please don't give your baby a pillow before the age of 18 months. The pillow may cover your baby's face and obstruct his breathing or cause overheating. Older babies can use the pillow as a step to climb up and fall out of the cot.

Blankets

You can use a blanket for a newborn until he starts rolling but once your baby starts rolling, NO BLANKET. A blanket is a suffocation risk. With newborns, they don't move around which means you can tuck the blanket in, to keep it safe. With babies older than 4 months or babies who are already rolling, we don't want to restrict their movements by tucking the blanket in. We want older babies to be able to move around and even start rolling onto their tummies. It's very safe for babies to sleep on their tummies if they got there by themselves. We ALWAYS put babies down on their backs but if they then roll onto their tummies, it's safe to leave them there. We never want to restrict babies' movements because it's part of their development and learning.

White noise and music

We **don't** want any music because music can become a sleep association. It helps a baby to go to sleep. We don't want anything **helping** your baby fall asleep. We want him to fall asleep **independently.**

The Nursery

White noise is allowed but only to **block external noise** like birds, trucks, dogs, a noisy toddler, or a busy street, **not to help** your baby sleep. If your baby's room isn't noisy, please remove the white noise so we can make the sleep arrangement as simple as possible.

If you do want to use white noise, you need to use a device that plays for **12 hours**. A lot of the white noise devices out there only play for 8 hours. You want to put your baby down in his cot at 7 pm, fully awake, with the white noise **on** so your baby can hear the white noise and fall asleep with the white noise. You want the white noise to play the whole night because if birds or trucks are a problem at 5 am, you don't want to get up to turn the white noise on. If you're out and about or have a baby who goes to day-care and is sensitive to noise, you can get a mobile white noise machine.

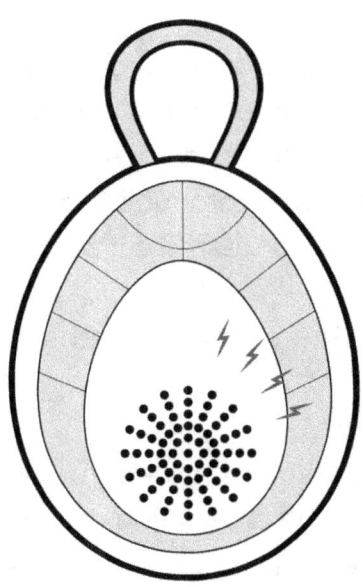

Night lights

We want your baby's nursery to be very dark which means **no** night light. I know when kids get a bit older (2.5 years and older) they genuinely can be afraid of the dark for some reason. Try to address the reason for the fear first.

- Kids who aren't sleeping well and who are **sleep-deprived** in general are more prone to fears.
- **Screen time** before bed can also be a big trigger for fears.

If you've addressed all the issues and your child is still scared, a very small night light is ok.

Dark room

Melatonin is a hormone produced in the brain and is often called the "sleep hormone" or the "darkness hormone". When the sun goes down and the darkness occurs, the pineal gland in the brain stimulates the production of melatonin. Melatonin makes us tired (time for rest). That's why we sleep at night.

During the day, the sun inactivates the production of melatonin.

Day sleeps: If a baby falls asleep in a very dark room, the brain will stimulate the production of melatonin. The quality and length of sleep will be so much better. If a baby wakes up from a short nap, opens his eyes, and can't see anything

The Nursery

(he can't focus on anything exciting), the chances he'll go back to sleep is a lot better.

<u>Night sleep:</u> I know overnight your baby's room will be dark, the problem is at bedtime during daylight savings. In a lot of places at 7 pm when your baby must go to bed, the room is still light. Your baby will find it very difficult to fall asleep.

<u>Early morning waking:</u> The slightest light change in the morning will trigger early morning waking. During daylight savings, it can become light as early as 5 am. Your baby will start waking up early. Keep your baby's room very dark up until 6:30 am.

<u>Ways to make the room dark:</u>
When I work with parents, I usually say, "During the **day** when you put your baby down in his cot, close the curtains/blinds and the door, you should not be able to see your hand. That's how dark I want the room." How can you do that?

- Block out curtains
- Block out blinds (but sometimes light can come through the sides)
- Window shutters (love these ☺)
- Aluminium tinfoil (quick solution)
- Nappy boxes in the window (quick solution)
- A black sheet over the window (quick solution)

Monitors

I love video monitors. I really like the monitors with a pan-tilt function because you can follow your baby in the cot.

When your baby is waking up from a nap or sleep overnight, watch him on the monitor first before rushing into the room. Most of the time, you'll see he's ok and trying to go back to sleep. If you run in there, he's going to get very excited to see you and wake himself up properly and it will take him a lot longer and a lot more effort to go back to sleep. I always recommend, if your baby wakes up and it isn't time for him to get up, watch him on the monitor to make sure he's safe and give him 10 minutes off crying to try and settle himself without you. If he's just tossing and turning, **leave him**. Don't go in.

Temperature

The recommended temperature for a nursery is 18 to 21 degrees Celsius. Babies like a **cooler** environment to sleep in rather than too warm.

Be careful not to overheat your baby with extra blankets and clothes. A good way to know if your baby is warm enough is to feel his face. Not his hands or feet. Most babies' hands and feet are cool. Babies' circulatory systems (blood supply systems) are still developing. Blood is shunted more often to vital organs and systems where it's needed most. His **hands and feet** are the last body parts to get a good blood supply.

Milk Feed and Solids

Breast or Bottle

Both are 100% fine. Yes, breastfeeding is the more natural choice, and it doesn't cost anything. It's good for your baby but, absolutely no pressure if you can't or don't want to breastfeed. It's your choice. Don't allow anyone (especially nurses—I'm a nurse too) to try and convince you otherwise. You do what you feel comfortable with.

I was so focused and adamant about breastfeeding my twins (and I really struggled), I didn't realise my son was not getting enough milk. He was crying all the time. At some point, my husband just gave him a bottle and he drank 100ml right there! He gulped it down and he was only 5 days old. I felt so bad for him and realised that it isn't about me wanting to breastfeed, it's about my babies. I must give them enough milk to grow, whether it's through formula or breastfeeding. If you don't have enough milk or it's causing too much stress, just give your baby a bottle with expressed milk or formula… it doesn't matter. It DOESN'T mean you've failed as a mum. Please. Do what is best for you and your baby.

Demand/Scheduled Feeding

Demand feeding is when you follow your baby's cues to show you when he's hungry which can be every hour or every 4 hours. My problem with demand feeding is it can easily start a snacking habit which doesn't help or promote sleep. Tiredness is then confused with hunger. The baby cries because he's tired, but you give him a feed because "babies are always hungry"—not true. I like scheduled feeding because you have a lot more control. When your baby is crying, it's a lot easier to eliminate why the baby is crying and not always assume it's hunger.

Example:
"My baby had a feed 2 hours ago (he can't be hungry). My baby just woke up from a nap (he can't be tired). Maybe the nappy is bothering him, that's why he's crying."

With scheduled feeding, I always recommend **3 hourly milk feeds** for a **newborn** up to 3 to 4 months old. The closer you get to **4 months**, try your best to be on a **4-hourly** feeding schedule. You'll see it will make life a lot easier and will give your baby an opportunity to sleep longer.

We always try to follow an EAT, PLAY, SLEEP schedule which means the milk feed is AFTER a sleep, not before.

The baby is fully awake and can have a proper feed. He isn't exhausted and trying to fall asleep on the feed. If you're going to continue feeding your baby before sleep and feed him to sleep, your baby is going to start associating milk with sleep and not, "I'm hungry I want milk." With newborns, it can be a bit difficult because their awake times are so short. When you must feed your baby before a nap, and always before bedtime, it's very important to keep your baby FULLY AWAKE for the feed and put him down AWAKE.

When you're bottle-feeding your baby, he should **never finish the bottle**. There should ALWAYS be something left in the bottle, then you know he had enough. If he starts finishing the bottle, next time add 30 to 50ml more milk.

Overnight feeding

At Happy Sleepers, when I work with babies from 0 to 7 months old, we still feed them overnight when they're hungry. Babies 7 months and older don't need to feed overnight. They need uninterrupted sleep more than milk. When you cut the overnight feeding, you'll notice a significant improvement in your baby's eating and drinking during the day.

If your baby is 0 to 7 months, it doesn't mean your baby isn't able to sleep through the night. In fact, I have a lot of babies 0 to 7 months who do sleep through the night. When a baby learned how to resettle and go back to sleep independently, when he wakes overnight and isn't hungry, he'll go back to sleep himself and sleep for a few more hours. Your baby will start skipping his overnight feeds HIMSELF. You're not going to stop his feedings for him. Follow my ACTION section for your baby's age. I will teach you, how to teach your baby. ☺

Solids

When your baby can sit up on his own in a highchair and is chewing or biting objects while looking at your food, he may be ready to start with solids. This can occur as early as 4 months.

Back in the day, we only started solids at 6 months, but that changed a few years ago to 4 months. All the books will say 6 months, unfortunately, they can't reprint all the books.

When you want to start solids, always start with **breakfast**. If there is an allergy to a food type, you'll be able to diagnose it during the day. We NEVER start a new food type at dinner. At dinner, we give food types you've given a few times and you know 100% there is no allergy.

Typical symptoms of a food allergy are:

- **Hives** or welts
- Flushed skin or rash
- Vomiting and/or diarrhea
- Face, tongue, or lip swelling (Go to the *emergency department* (ED) immediately!)
- Coughing or wheezing (Go to the ED immediately!)
- Difficulty breathing (Go to the ED immediately!)
- **Loss of consciousness** (Go to the ED immediately!)

Milk Feed and Solids

<u>Feeding Examples:</u> (If your baby has a long nap in the morning or afternoon, please don't wake him for a milk feed. Feed him when he wakes.)

<u>Babies 0 to 4 months:</u>
Give milk every 3 hours (7 am, 10 am, 1 pm, 4 pm, 7 pm). Only **5** feeds during the day and 1 or 2 feeds overnight.

<u>Babies 4 months to 10 months:</u>
Milk feeds every 4 hours (7 am, 11 am, 3 pm, 7 pm). Only **4** feeds during the day, solids in between and 1 or no feeds overnight. At 7 am we have **milk first** then solids 30 minutes later

> **7 am:** Milk + breakfast (30 minutes to 1 hour after the milk)
> **11 am:** Milk
> **1 pm:** Lunch
> **3 pm:** Milk
> **5:30 pm:** Dinner
> **6:45 pm:** Milk

<u>Babies 11 to 13/14 months</u> **(2 naps):**
Milk feeds every 4 hours and solids in between. No overnight feeds. At 7 am we have **solids first** then milk 30 minutes later. At this age solids become a bit more important at this age. We don't want your baby to fill his body up with milk and then not want the solids.

7 am: Breakfast + Milk (30 minutes to 1 hour after)
11 am: Milk
1 pm: Lunch
3 pm: Milk
5:30 pm: Dinner
6:45 pm: Milk

<u>Babies 14 months and older **(1 nap)**:</u>
Milk feeds every 6 to 8 hours and solids in between. No overnight feeds. At 7 am we have **solids first** then milk 30 minutes later. At this age solids become a bit more important at this age. We don't want your baby to fill his body up with milk and then not want the solids.

7 am: Breakfast + milk (30 minutes to 1 hour after breakfast).
9:30 am: Snack
11 am: Lunch
3 pm: Snack
5:30 pm: Dinner
6:45 pm: Milk

Dream feeding

Dream feeding is a thing that started a few years back and has become very popular. A dream feed is when you're feeding your baby while he's still fast asleep around 10 pm.

Milk Feed and Solids

The idea is to top him up with milk to extend his overnight sleep but it doesn't always work because it's not always hunger that wakes babies up overnight, it's the inability to resettle and go back to sleep INDEPENDENTLY. Sleeping longer blocks overnight or sleeping through the night is a learned skill. Yes, if you give your baby enough food during the day, it can prevent him from waking up hungry overnight, but even if you do feed him enough during the day, and he hasn't learned the sleep skill yet, he's still going to wake overnight. If your baby is 6 months and younger, you should still feed him overnight if he's hungry (not to help him to go back to sleep) but babies 7 months and older don't need feeds overnight.

The problem with a dream feed is, we all must go through REM sleep overnight to feel rested in the morning. When you decide you want to feed your baby at 10 pm because you're ready to go to bed, your baby might be in REM sleep. This means you're interrupting his normal sleep cycle and making him more tired. It's better to wait until your baby wakes up naturally when he's hungry.

Happy Sleepers

Sleeping Bags and Swaddles

Newborns: You must swaddle your newborn baby because swaddling protects your baby against their natural startle reflex which means better sleep. The **Moro reflex**, or **startle reflex**, refers to an involuntary motor response that infants develop shortly after birth. A **startle reflex** may involve the **infant** suddenly splaying their arms and moving their legs before bringing their arms in front of their body.

Happy Sleepers

If your baby keeps startling, it will affect their sleep. If your baby is 0 to 4.5 months and not rolling yet, and you can clearly see he still has a startle reflex, you must swaddle him. The startle reflex usually goes away when they start rolling, which is around the 4.5-month mark. If your baby is still a newborn and not in a swaddle, I highly recommend getting one.

I know a lot of parents say that their baby really doesn't like the swaddle, or they just don't want to swaddle their baby but if you want to improve your baby's sleep, you unfortunately, have to. I have worked with a lot of babies where we put them back into the swaddles and they slept so much better.

I know a lot of parents swaddle their baby's arms UP, but that swaddling doesn't work well because with their arms up they can still startle and wake your baby from their sleep.

Sleeping Bags and Swaddles

Swaddling a baby with their arms DOWN works a lot better. When the arms are against the body, the startle will not wake your baby. The whole point of swaddling a baby is to improve sleep. The arms must be down. It doesn't matter what brand swaddle you use, but the arms must be down. You can use a normal Muslin wrap, fold it in a triangle and wrap your baby's arms tight. With a Muslin wrap, your baby can't move his arms at all, they are quite restrained.

You can also use swaddle sleeping bags. With the swaddle sleeping bags, your baby can still move their arms inside. If he wants to bring his hands up and suck on his fingers to soothe himself that way, it's fine because the arms are still against the body, and he can't startle himself awake.

Happy Sleepers

When your baby starts rolling, you can transition him out of that swaddle. You start by taking only one arm out (usually the dominant arm if you know which one it is) for a week and then you take the other arm out.

Sleeping Bags and Swaddles

When your baby is little, it doesn't really matter which sleeping bag you're using (the bag one or the one with the separated legs) but it does matter when your baby is older.

When your child is 16 months and older, I recommend the one with the bag at the bottom. When a baby is still in a cot, we always use sleeping bags to keep babies warm overnight but when babies are older, we're also using the sleeping bag to restrict them from lifting their legs up. When babies get older, they get tall enough to lift their legs high enough and jump (or fall) out of the cot. They start doing this at an age when they are not necessarily ready to transition to a bed, but parents do because they're scared the baby is going to get hurt. When we're using sleeping bags at this age, we're making it difficult for your baby to lift his leg high enough to actually get out. I usually don't move babies out of their cots before the age of 2.5 to 3 years. Read more about this in the toddler section.

Screen Time

Improving sleep at night, you must avoid any screen time at least 1 to 2 hours before bedtime. The blue screen from the devices blocks melatonin production which means there is no hormone helping your baby feel more tired and getting ready to sleep.

In general, screen time can also disrupt calm, peaceful sleep. I remember when Anthony was a baby, he couldn't watch Peppa Pig before bed (can you believe it!). Peppa Pig caused him to wake up crying overnight. I had to stop Peppa Pig. Kids can be very sensitive to screen time and processes it a lot different than adults. Be careful what your toddler is watching in the afternoon.

Teething

As a sleep specialist, I hear this a lot, "My baby isn't sleeping because he's teething." Well, teething can be the reason, but it isn't ALWAYS the reason. Usually, when a baby is teething, there are more tears involved and the baby, in general, isn't feeling well. Because mum is feeling sorry for the baby, she starts to rock or pat him, give extra milk overnight, give the dummy more often, or any other coping mechanism. When the teething is over, the baby doesn't want to give up the extra attention he had when he was teething (which is very normal) and he'll demand it until he gets it. There the vicious cycle starts, and you don't know how to stop it. When a baby is teething, what you need to do is the following:

- Give your baby pain relief (like baby Nurofen) 30 minutes **BEFORE** bed. If you don't give the pain relief and your baby is really teething, he will wake up over night in pain. You're going to give the pain relief in anyway then, you might as well do it before bed which means he doesn't have broken sleep

overnight. Give the Nurofen before bed and he's covered for the night.
- Give teething gel (like SM33) to numb the gums.
- When your baby cries overnight, wait a few minutes (10 minutes) to see if he can resettle himself back to sleep. If he can't, give the pain medication again (after 4 to 6 hours) because he has NO pain relief in his body. He needs a top up.
- Don't start rocking or patting your baby if you didn't do it before. You're going to keep doing it even if your baby isn't teething anymore because he loves it!
- Don't give milk overnight after 7 months. Babies don't need overnight feeding after 7 months, they need SLEEP and teething certainly doesn't make them thirstier overnight.
- Don't start co-sleeping. Your baby doesn't need co-sleeping now. He is sleeping better in his cot. If you start co-sleeping, it will take you 2 weeks to get him out again.

How do I know my baby is teething?
- Pain
- Runny stools
- **Rosy cheeks**
- Fever
- Drooling
- Crankiness
- Hands keep going to the mouth.

You can run your finger along the front edges of the gums. You'll feel swollen ridges of pre-teething gums.

Teething

The drug of choice for teething is always Nurofen because Nurofen has anti-inflamatory ingredients which helps with swelling. Parents always think that Nurofen is stronger than Panadol, it isn't. It works differently and is more effective. SM33 is also a good teething gel.

Other things you can do to relief the pain:

- Give your baby a frozen teething ring or rubber
- Rub your baby's gums with your finger or a wet gauze
- Give him frozen fruit or icy pole

70% of babies get their teeth according to this guideline:

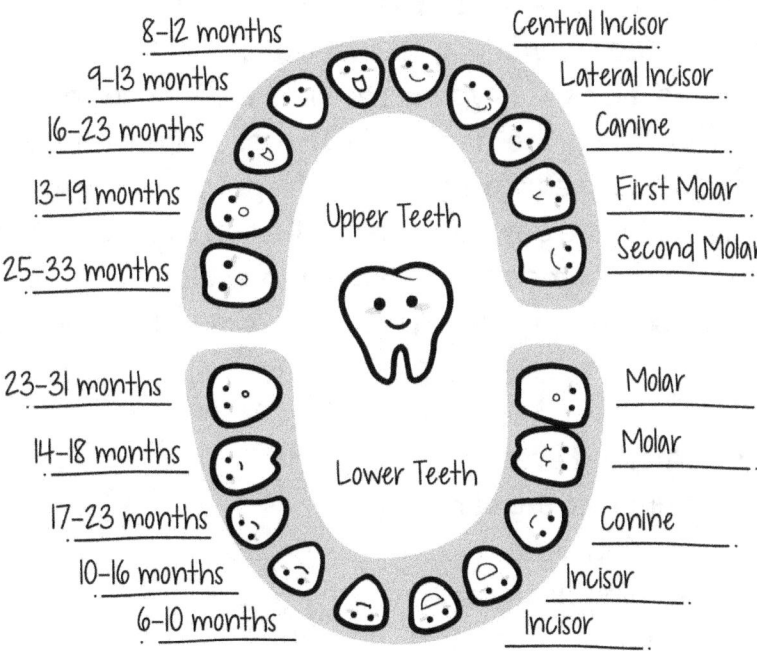

Teething can be very challenging!

Tired Signs

OVERTIREDNESS makes it very difficult for a baby to fall asleep. Don't make your baby overtired. When a baby is overtired, they're working themselves up instead of down. They almost look like hyperactive children. Making your baby overtired during the day will NOT make him sleep better overnight. Sleep encourages more sleep. The more your baby sleeps during the day, the better he'll sleep overnight. Please look at awake times (next section) to avoid overtiredness. Here are some signs to help you recognise when your baby is tired:

- Rubbing eyes
- Pulling of the ears
- Closing fists
- Arching backward
- Yawning

Awake Time

Awake times between naps and bedtime are extremely important (especially with newborns) to prevent overtiredness. When a baby is overtired, they work themselves **up** instead of down and then it can be very difficult to get your baby down for a nap and it goes along with a lot of crying. Overtiredness, especially in the newborn phase, is your biggest enemy. **Avoid it at all costs**.

As your baby gets older, they'll need more awake time and because of that, the number of naps will gradually fall away. We always **aim** for babies to **fall asleep within 10 minutes** of crying. Whenever it takes your baby **more than 10 minutes** to fall asleep (once he/she is sleep trained), next time he'll need 5 or 10 more minutes MORE awake time.

We always work on **awake time**, we never work on **actual time** but we also follow proper tired signs.

Example:
For a 7-month-old baby, their awake time between naps and bedtime is **usually** (not always) between 2.5 to 3.5 hours. The awake time is usually **less in the morning** and as the day progresses, your baby will need more awake time. Usually 2.5 hours in the morning, maybe 3 hours before his second nap, and then 3.5 hours before bed.

We always work on **awake time**, we never work on **actual time.**

If your baby doesn't show you proper tired signs it might be better to follow awake time but if your baby does show you proper tired signs, it's better to use tired signs. What I mean by that is, if your baby always looks tired at the 2.5-hour mark and he falls asleep within less than 10 minutes, that's good. But then one morning, your baby looks tired at the 2-hour mark, put your baby down. You don't have to wait for 2.5 hours to pass before you put him down, but you have to make sure he shows proper tired signs. Don't put him down if he only yawned once. Once he's in the cot, **he's in the cot to stay**, you can't then decide, "Oh my goodness, he isn't tired enough," and take him out of the cot. That's going to confuse your baby. Putting your baby down prematurely will go along with more crying.

Another example:
Your baby wakes up at 6:30 am. You count for example 2.5 hours from 6:30 am for your baby's first nap which is 9 am. If your baby wakes at 6 am and you couldn't get him back to sleep, his first nap will be at 8:30 am, not 9 am.

Awake Time

If your baby has 3 naps, for the first 2 naps you **NEVER** wake him. Let him sleep. For the last nap of the day, you always wake him according to his awake time. If your baby's awake time is 3 hours at the end of the day, your baby must be woken up at 4 pm for a 7 pm bedtime. If he naturally wakes up at 3:30 pm from the nap, bedtime will be at 6:30 pm. Remember, we work on awake time, not actual time. Bedtime will not always be 7 pm. It depends on what time your baby wakes up from his last nap.

Once your baby is in the cot, **he's in the cot to stay**, you can't then decide, "Oh my goodness, he isn't tired enough," and take him out of the cot. That will cause a lot of confusion.

Here is the maximum awake timetable for each age:

Happy Sleepers

Maximum awake time between naps — Happy Sleepers
Sound sleep for everyone

0 - 12 Weeks

Awake time BETWEEN NAPS: 45 Minutes - 1.5 Hour

12 Weeks - 4.5 Months

Awake time BETWEEN NAPS: 1.5 Hours - 2 Hours

4.5 Months - 7 Months
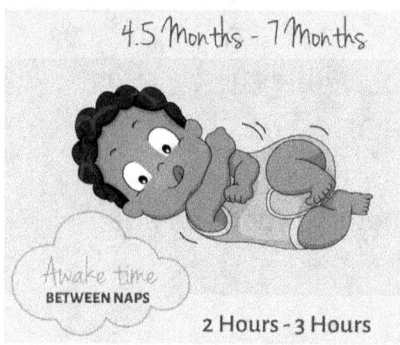
Awake time BETWEEN NAPS: 2 Hours - 3 Hours

7 Months - 13 Months

Awake time BETWEEN NAPS: 3 Hours - 4 Hours

13 Months - 2.5 Years

Awake time BETWEEN NAPS: 4 Hours - 5.5 Hours

2.5 Years - 4 Years

Awake time BETWEEN NAPS: 5.5 Hours - 12 Hours

Awake Time

Here are a few examples:

Example

7 am: Wake
9 am: First Nap (2 hours awake time)
10:30 am: Wake (Baby slept for 1.5 hrs)
12:45 pm: Second Nap
           (2 hours 15 min awake time)
1:30 pm: Wake (Baby slept for 45 min)
4 pm: Third Nap (2 hours 30 min awake time)
4:30 pm: Wake baby
6:30 pm: Bedtime Routine
7 pm: Bed

You've got this!

Last Nap

1 hr awake time: Wake baby at 6pm
1.5 hr awake time: Wake baby at 5.30pm
2 hr awake time: Wake baby at 5pm
2.5 hr awake time: Wake baby at 4:30pm
3 hr awake time: Wake baby at 4pm
3.5 hr awake time: Wake baby at 3:30pm
4 hr awake time: Wake baby at 3pm
4.5 hr awake time: Wake baby at 2:30pm
5 hr awake time: Wake baby at 2pm
5.5 hr awake time: Wake baby at 1:30pm

You've got this!

Awake times gradually increase over time which means the nap will gradually fall away because there is not enough time in the day for that nap anymore. Some babies might have less naps because they have long naps (2.5 – 4 hour naps) which is absolutely fine. Here is an example when babies have how many naps.

0 – 4 months: 3 – 4 naps a day
4 months – 6.5 months: 3 naps a day
6.5 months – 13 months: 2 naps a day
13 months – approxamately 2.5 – 3 years: 1 nap a day

Sleep Associations

A "sleep prop" is something external (like a dummy, rocking to sleep, patting to sleep, or feeding to sleep) a baby needs to fall asleep.

Ok, are you paying attention? What I'm about to tell you is the most important piece of information you will need in order to get your baby to start sleeping straight through the night! Here it's:

Your baby is a poor sleeper because he relies on external help (sleep associations) to help him fall asleep and to help him stay asleep. If you want your baby/toddler to be a good sleeper you want to teach him **proper sleep skills.** You want to teach him how to **fall asleep** INDEPENDENTLY and you want to teach him how to **stay asleep** INDEPENDENTLY. When anyone, baby, toddler or adult can do that, that person has an internalised skill to sleep. Like you do – I'm sure ☺. You don't need someone to pat your back or rock you to sleep. You can do it yourself, but your baby can't. He needs someone to HELP him to sleep by giving him a dummy, or feed him to sleep or rock him to sleep or whatever. He needs something from someone to HELP him to go to sleep or resettle back to sleep and that's what needs to change. You MUST REMOVE ALL HELP and teach your baby an internalise skill. It literally takes one night to teach your baby this skill and then it's just practise. If your baby isn't able to fall asleep in less than 10 min and sleep at least 4 – 6 hour blocks (0 – 6.5 months) or sleep through the night (7 months and older) in a week, then you didn't remove all the sleep associations. Something is still present.

Teach your baby an internalised skill to sleep, so he knows how to fall asleep and stay asleep independently and he'll be an amazing sleeper for the rest of his life.

Examples of sleep associations:
1. Rocking to sleep
2. Patting to sleep
3. Swaying to sleep
4. Walking to sleep
5. Bouncing to sleep
6. Holding your baby's hand or letting him hold yours
7. Co-sleeping (he needs your presence to help him go to sleep)
8. Stroking to sleep
9. Dummy
10. Anything where there is motion involved to HELP your baby to fall asleep

Sleep Associations

We want to remove all external help and teach your baby, an internalised skill to sleep, so he knows how to fall asleep and stay asleep independently. If you're to continue with even a little bit of a pat (just a tiny one), your child will never learn how to fall asleep independently. So please, when we start the program, we need you to remove all the sleep associations **cold turkey**.

Rocking and Patting

Now we're going to talk about a difficult one. **NO MORE** walking to sleep, patting to sleep swaying to sleep, rocking to sleep, bouncing to sleep, anything where there's motion involved. We must remove ALL external help and teach your baby an internalised skill to sleep. We want him to know how to fall asleep and stay asleep independently. If you're still going continue with even a little bit of a pat, your child will never learn how to sleep independently. Think for yourself, when you want to go to sleep, do you need someone to pat you on the back to go to sleep? It will definitely be nice ☺ but you don't NEED it (like your baby) to help you to go to sleep. We want to teach your baby the same skill but unfortunately ALL external help (how insignificantly it might feel or sound) MUST GO!

Dummies

Now we're going to talk about a big one. If your baby doesn't have a dummy, PLEASE never ever start one. If your baby has a dummy and you want to improve his sleep, unfortunately, we must remove it. Dummies and feeding to sleep, are 2 of the biggest sleep associations out there.

For example: If you're starting your program tonight, you can give your baby his dummy the whole day but at the bedtime routine, I need you to get all your hundreds of dummies together, and chuck them inside the bin, **gone forever**.

We aren't even going to use the dummy during the day because it's just going to confuse your baby. When we teach your baby an internalised skill to sleep, he isn't going to need that dummy ever again. He will have an internalised skill to fall asleep and stay asleep independently, and that's what we want for him. So please, I know this is a big one for a lot of parents, but please trust me, it's a lot easier than you think. And yes, I have had a few parents who tried to give back the dummy after the sleep training, but the baby just spat it out, they didn't want it anymore. Please just trust me, this will be the best thing for your child.

Comforters:
Your baby can have a comforter. Comforters aren't sleep associations. Try to give your baby a comforter that doesn't have a blanket attached to it. Your baby might fall asleep with the blanket over his face which will make him uncomfortable.

Sleep Associations

Holding his hand or stroking to sleep

Holding your baby's hand or stroking him to sleep is also a big sleep association. He needs that touch to **help** him go to sleep and what we want to do is get rid of all the **help** so he can do it by himself. This section can involve other things as well like:

- Baby holds mum's hand or finger
- Baby wants to hold mum's hair or ear
- Baby wants to hold on to mum's toe
- Mum must stroke baby's back or forehead

Feeding to sleep

Feeding to sleep is one of the biggest sleep associations because it's sooooo easy to do. If your baby is crying, put him on the boob and he'll fall asleep instantly. What makes it even nicer is the skin-to-skin touch. Yes, feeding and skin-to-skin touch are very important for bonding but feeding your baby to sleep is going to cause a big sleep problem for you. The thing is, if you're going to feed your baby to sleep all the time, he's going to associate feeding with going to sleep and not with, "I'm going to drink because I'm hungry." Like I said before, if you need to feed your baby to sleep at bedtime, he's going to need to feed to sleep overnight every single time he wakes up and will be unable to go back to sleep himself. Is he hungry every time he wakes up? No! But you taught him if he wants to sleep, he needs a feed.

Obviously, you can still breastfeed your baby when you do sleep training, but you need to stop feeding to sleep. Keep him FULLY AWAKE while you're feeding him and then put him down fully awake. When you follow an EAT-PLAY-SLEEP routine, you will not have this problem because you'll feed your baby after sleeping, not before. The only time will be before bed at night. The same goes for overnight feeds. Keep your baby fully awake and put him down fully awake after the feed. The same rules apply to a bottle-fed baby. Keep him fully awake while feeding. Don't allow your baby to close their eyes for one second. He'll have a mini micro nap while he has his eyes closed and then the process of putting him down for the night will go along with a lot of crying because he just had a mini micro nap.

Car rides and pram rides

Car rides and pram rides **helps** your baby fall asleep. The movement in the car or pram slightly "rocks" your baby to sleep, which is a sleep association, BUT life goes on. We

Sleep Associations

can't stay at home all the time. Your baby will and must sleep in the car or pram otherwise it will affect your mental health. You must get out of the house. Your baby can't have all his sleep in the cot. Yes, it will be good for his quality sleep, but it isn't sustainable. The main thing is your baby must learn how to sleep and self-settle in the cot first then the occasional sleep in the car or pram will not affect his ability to self-settle when he goes back into the cot again. If your baby needs the car or pram to go to sleep, then it's a problem.

Tapping the mattress or rocking the cot

This is a big sleep school thing where you tap the baby's bum, and then you slowly move your hand and tap the mattress. The tapping sound **helps** the baby go to sleep. The other thing they do is physically shake the cot which results in you sort of rocking the baby to sleep without you touching him. You can also do that with a bassinette. You slightly shake the cot to "rock" the baby to sleep. You can also get bassinettes that have a motor, and the bassinette moves all the time. All these "methods" or equipment **HELPS** your baby to sleep. They are EXTERNAL STRATEGIES. We want to get rid of ALL external strategies and teach your baby an INTERNALISED skill so he can self-settle.

Co-sleeping

Co-sleeping is a very difficult and sensitive subject because so many parents choose to co-sleep but then there are also many who are forced into co-sleeping because of sleep deprivation. Co-sleeping is a practice in which babies and young children sleep close to their parents in the same bed rather than sleeping separately in different beds. In many cultures around the world, babies and adults have always slept together. In fact, sleeping separately is a relatively new concept that instilled itself into Western culture in the 19th century.

If you and your baby are sleeping well in one bed and everyone in the family is getting good quality sleep for a big portion of the night, I'm not here to tell you that you're not allowed to co-sleep. I'm a deep sleeper and I always felt uncomfortable with the idea of co-sleeping. Whether it's a cultural, bonding, or sleep deprivation reason why you want to co-sleep, SIDS is always a reality. You must make sure that you co-sleep safely.

Unfortunately, in terms of sleep training or improving your baby's sleep, you can't do it while you're co-sleeping. Your baby must be in his own bassinette/cot in your room or preferably in his own room. I truly believe you and your baby will get the best quality sleep if you're in separate beds. Co-sleeping is also a sleep association. Your baby needs your closeness to fall asleep.

Pickups

When we do sleep training with babies 4.5 months and older, we DON'T pick them up at all. Once he's in the cot, he's in the cot to stay. Pickups aren't sleep associations, but it's very stimulating. Every single time you pick your baby up, you can add 5 to 15 minutes to his settling time. This means it's going to take him longer to fall asleep, meaning a lot more crying, and we want to limit the amount of crying as much as possible.

When you put your baby down in the cot, everything must be perfect. Consider the following:

- Your baby must be tired enough
- Your baby must be fully fed, especially at bedtime
- His nappy must be dry
- He must be comfortable which means no pain. If your baby is teething, you must give pain relief 30 minutes before you put him down for the nap or even at bedtime.

There are only a few reasons when it's reasonable to pick him up:

- Overnight for feeding (0 – 7 months)
- Your baby vomited and you must clean him up.
- Your baby has a soiled nappy, and you must change it.
- Your baby needs medication and it's difficult for you to give it in the cot. Put your baby down on the changing table. Don't cuddle him in your arms.
- Your baby is unwell.

Even overnight, don't pick him up unless you have a good reason (like mentioned above). If you're going to pick your baby up overnight for no reason, he will start waking up overnight to be picked up. He likes the attention.

<u>Babies 0 to 4.5 months (Limited pickups)</u>
If your baby is a newborn, yes you can pick him up, but please try to limit the pickups as much as possible. It's still stimulating, and it will extend the settling time. When you pick your baby up, bring him to your shoulder and only walk with him until he's calm. Don't rock him with your legs and don't pat him on the bum (sleep associations). Just walk with him until he's calm (still crying a little bit) and then put him down (still fully awake).

Twins

Having twins can be (and was for me) VERY overwhelming. Suddenly you have two little human beings, both wants your attention at the same time. They're hungry at the same time; they're tired at the same time, and they're sick at the same time and you as a parent only have one pair of arms. If you have a partner who is at home all the time, that's the perfect scenario because then your partner can take one baby and you can take the other, but 9/10 times that isn't the case. You might have their help in the late afternoon and at night but during the day, you'll most probably be by yourself, which makes it even more important for you to get organised and have a routine and structure from the very beginning. Having babies who can go down easily for sleep without much effort and are well-rested is very important for parents with multiples.

When we work with twins, we try our best to treat them as individual babies because they do have individual needs, but it isn't always possible. As a twin mum, my biggest fear was always that one twin would wake the other one up and yes, a lot of the times it did happen. But for me, sometimes one twin would scream his/her head off and the other one would be right next to him/her but didn't wake up at all. Sometimes they would get used to one another's cries and wouldn't wake up.

When we want to sleep train twins, there are a few things to consider:

- Unfortunately, you must separate them while you're doing sleep training. You can't do it in the same room because, as I said before, you don't want one twin to wake the other one up. To sleep train them properly, you have to wait a few minutes of crying to see if your baby will self-settle before you go in. If they're in the same room, you're going to jump into that room to try and prevent that. Once they're sleep trained, you can put them back together.
- When you separate them, you can also use white noise in each baby's room to block out the other one crying a bit more.
- At Happy Sleepers, we prefer the "camp out method" where you sit right next to your baby until he/she falls asleep. That might be possible for you at night when you have your partner at home but during the day if you're alone, unfortunately, the camp out method will not be possible. You'll have to do "responsive settling" where you go in and out of the room. When we work with twins, we always **put them down 5 minutes apart.**

Twins

- We always try to treat twins as individual babies because then they'll get into a structured routine more quickly, but it can be very difficult for a twin parent if the babies are sleeping at different times and different lengths. If one baby has an hour nap in the morning and the other baby has an hour and a half it can still be manageable but if one baby had 30 minutes and the other one had 2 hours, they'll be on completely different schedules. This means you don't get a break because they'll be awake at different times. My recommendation is to leave them for a few days and see what they do. Most of the time, they do get into sync, and they usually wake within 20 minutes of each other. But if they don't it can becomes very difficult for you. My recommendation is, if one baby wakes from a nap or overnight feed and the other baby isn't awake within 15 - 20 minutes, wake him.
- When I work with twins, there is usually a good sleeper or a better sleeper and then the "troublemaker" ☺. It's always best to sleep train both at the same time, so you only need to follow one schedule and one way to put them down. It's already difficult to raise two babies at the same time, try to make it as easy for yourself as possible.

Part 3:

Action

A Step-by-Step Guide On How to Improve Your Baby/Toddlers' Sleep According to Age Group

Newborn (0 to 4.5 months)

Introduction:

Before we start with your plan and how we're going to improve your baby's sleep, I just want to say something. Your baby is very young, please don't put a lot of pressure on yourself or your baby. Yes, I understand you're tired, and you want to improve your baby's sleep, but it takes time and practice. If you don't get it "right" the first time, then you try again tomorrow, for example, in the plan, I asked: "Please never feed your baby to sleep" because it's a massive sleep association BUT your baby is sooooo little, it's almost impossible to keep them awake while they're feeding and it's going to take a lot of effort from you to keep him awake.

I want you to have a certain mindset with a newborn: "I'm practising." Think, "Every time I feed my baby, I'm going to try my best not to feed him to sleep but if he does, it's ok and I will try again the next feed." The first 4 months are practice. Everything I recommend in this plan you're going to practice but when you get to 4 months, it's very important not to feed your baby to sleep. Please try to relax, nothing must be perfect, and nothing will be perfect in the first 4 months. Enjoy your baby.

The big difference between a newborn and babies 4.5 months and older is:

- You're still in the learning and practicing phase
- 3-hourly feeds
- You're allowed to pick your baby up
- You can wait 5 minutes of crying during the day instead of 10 minutes of crying
- Your baby will be in a swaddle instead of a sleeping bag

Newborn (0 to 4.5 months)

Awake time:

Please read Page 95 again about awake times

Daytime Routine:

When we work with babies 4 months and older, we usually follow a 7 am to 7 pm schedule. We pick them up at 7 am, and we usually put them down around 7 pm. But with a newborn, nothing is strict. There is a lot more flexibility. With newborns, we usually follow an 8 am to 9 pm routine. Picking your baby up at 8 am and putting him down at 9 pm. The reason why we do that is so mum can have more sleep. She has just gone through a pregnancy, she's tired, it's hard work taking care of a newborn. Mum needs maximum sleep.

If we follow a 7 am to 7 pm schedule with a newborn, there is almost no chance mum will go to bed at 7 pm. But if you put your baby down at 9 pm and your baby just had a feed, there is a better chance that you will go to bed at 9 pm. That means you'll win an extra 2 hours of sleep before the next feed. If you want more sleep for yourself, I highly recommend an 8 am to 9 pm routine. But if a 7 am to 7 pm schedule is going to suit your family better, that's 100% ok. Usually, from 4 months, we change to 7 am to 7 pm.

0 to 4 months (8 am to 9 pm) with 3 hourly feeds
8:00 am – Wake (7 am from 4 months)
If your baby is still asleep at 8:00 am, please wake him.
He needs structure and routine in his day. We also need 12 hours during the day to fit in all the naps and 5x feeds.

Newborn (0 to 4.5 months)

8:15 am – Milk feed
Milk feed every 3 hours (8 am, 11 am, 2 pm, 5 pm, 8 pm, top-up at 8:45 pm). If your baby is still asleep at the feeding time, please don't wake him for the feed. He'll wake himself when he's very hungry, EXCEPT if he had a very long nap and hasn't had a feed for 4 hours. Then you will wake him. Next feed will still be the original time.

Approximately 8:45 am – Nap
Your baby needs 3 to 4 naps per day

2nd, 3rd and 4th Nap
Times depends on the length of the naps and awake times thereafter. You must work it out.
Your baby must be awake at 8 pm for a 9 pm (depending on age and awake time)

8:30 pm – Start his bedtime routine

9:00 pm – Bedtime

From 4 months (7 am to 7 pm) and 4 hourly feeds

7:00 am – Wake
If your baby is still asleep at 7:00 am, please wake him. He needs structure and routine in his day. We also need 12 hours during the day to fit in all the naps and 4x feeds.

7:15 am – Milk feed + solids
Milk feed every 4 hours (7 am, 11 am, 3 pm, 7 pm). If your baby is still asleep at the feeding time, please don't wake him for the feed. He'll wake himself if he's very hungry.

> **Approximately 9:00/9:30 am** – 1st Nap
> Your baby needs 3 naps per day
> **2nd, 3rd, and 4th Nap**
> These nap times depend on the length of the previous nap and awake times thereafter. You must work it out.
> **Your baby must be awake at 5:00 pm for a 7 pm bedtime**
> 6:30 pm – Start his bedtime routine
> 7:00 pm – Bedtime

Bedtime Routine:

I always recommend for the bedtime routine to be in the room where your baby is going to sleep. I know your baby is still very little which means it isn't a big deal at this stage, but it's good to start healthy habits and routine early. What happens later, when your baby gets older, when you do the milk and story, say in the lounge, and now you're walking to your baby's room to put him down for the night, it's almost like walking to **jail**. Anxiety builds up. More crying happens. There is no positive relationship with his nursery because your baby feels it's only a place where you dump him for sleep.

What we want is for your baby to have a positive relationship with his nursery. Once he has his bath, walk straight to the nursery, dress him in there, give him milk, read a story, or sing

Newborn (0 to 4.5 months)

a song (no playing), give attention. It's all positive and nice. Once your baby finishes the feed, put him in the swaddle and straight into the cot. No time for anxiety.

The bedtime routine should only be **30 minutes**. Try not to extend it any longer. I know 30 minutes sounds very short, but it's possible. If your baby takes a long time to drink, have a very short bath. As he gets better with the drinking, he can start having a longer bath.

<u>0 to 4 months:</u>
   8:30 pm – Bath
   Dress in Pyjamas
   Milk feed + sing (keep your baby wide awake)
   Swaddle
   9:00 pm – Cot (awake)

<u>4 to 4.5 months:</u>
   6:30 pm – Bath
   Dress in pyjamas
   Milk feed + story (keep your baby wide awake)
   Swaddle/sleeping bag
   (When your baby starts rolling, no more swaddle, change to sleeping bag)
   7:00 pm – Cot (awake)

Reflux babies:
If you have a reflux baby or a baby who is prone to vomiting, we usually swap the bath and the feed so there is more time for the milk to be digested.

> ### 0 to 4 months:
> **8:30 pm** – Feed
> Bath
> Dress in pyjamas
> Sing (keep your baby wide awake)
> Swaddle
> **9:00 pm** – Cot (awake)

Bedtime
(Night 1 to 3):

Let's start the process—good luck! You can do this! Remember, you're going to give your baby the GIFT OF SLEEP FOR THE REST OF HIS LIFE. Don't focus on the crying now. Don't allow the crying to run with your emotions. All babies cry. I have never worked with a baby who doesn't cry. It's VERY NORMAL for them to sound almost hysterical. They don't have the capability yet to regulate their cries properly. They go from 0 to 100 in seconds, but they also go from 100 to 0 in seconds.

Your baby will resist the change. Babies don't like change. They want things to stay the same, they don't know any better, but you do.

Newborn (0 to 4.5 months)

LET'S DO IT!

You've done your bedtime routine; your baby is in his cot, and he immediately starts crying. It's ok, your baby is fine. Walk across to the door, close it, switch off the light.

- ♥ **Sit beside the cot**. Have some calming music in your ears to calm you down (earphones).
- ♥ Say repetitive key phrases ("Night-night-time" or "It's sleepy time now").
- ♥ You can occasionally touch him on the shoulder **(for 3 seconds ONLY and then lift your hand up. Don't leave your hand on his body).** We don't want this to become a new external strategy he uses to fall asleep. Remember, it isn't your job to put him to sleep; you're only there to offer some comfort. It must be his job now to put himself to sleep.
- ♥ If he gets really worked up, **you can pick him up**, walk around the room until he's calm. NO ROCKING with your legs and NO PATTING with your hand on his bum. Be VERY careful. He isn't allowed to fall asleep on your shoulder. If he calms down but is still crying a little bit, put him down. **He must fall asleep in the cot.** Try not to pick him up too often. He must be inside his cot more often than in your arms. If you can get yourself not to pick him up at all, don't.
- ♥ Do all this until he falls asleep. **No time limit.** (Babies at this age can easily cry for 45 to 90 minutes ☹).
- ♥ Once he's asleep, wait 5 minutes and then leave the room.

Overnight Waking and Feeding:

- **9 pm to 12 am:** If your baby wakes between 9 pm and 12 pm you're going to **settle your baby**. NO FEEDING. You're only going to feed your baby 3 hourly overnight, not every time he wakes up.
Wait **10 minutes** of full-on crying (not whining or grizzling) before you respond to him at all. This will delay the gratification and prevent him from becoming more stimulated upon seeing you.

  If he's still protesting after 10 minutes, go in and repeat the same strategies you were using at bedtime. Stay with him and say your key phrases until he goes back to sleep. NO FEEDING.

  - Repeat the same process each time he wakes before the 3 hourly feeding mark.

- **12 am and after (3 hourly feeds):** We do 3 hourly feeds overnight when your baby wakes himself. You don't have to wake your baby at the 3 hourly marks unless medically indicated.
  - Wait **10 minutes** of full-on crying (not whining or grizzling) before you respond to him at all. You must wait the 10 minutes before the feed (even if you know he's hungry) because he might surprise you and go back to sleep. If he's still crying at the 10-minute mark, go in, pick him up, **change the nappy first.** This is to delay the gratification of the night-time feeds. Your baby will be less likely to connect waking and crying with feeding.

Newborn (0 to 4.5 months)

- ♥ Keep an eye on him through the feed and do your best to **keep him awake**.
- ♥ He must go back to his cot awake.
- ♥ Please keep him in his room at night.
- ♥ Keep the lights low and your voice quiet.
- ♥ Night-time is for sleeping, resist the urge to watch TV. This will also help you resettle faster when you get back to your own bed.
- ♥ Don't consider morning anything before 7:30 am. Make a big deal about it being morning and take him out of the bedroom for his first feed (6:30 am from 4 months).

The 10-minute rules:
- He must cry full-on for 10 minutes. We don't count whining, grizzling, or blowing raspberries.
- If he cries for 4 minutes and he stops for **more than 1 minute**, you must restart the 10 minutes again.
- You must wait the **full 10 minutes**. A lot of babies cry for 9.5 minutes and then they resettle and go back to sleep for another 1 - 3 hours.
- If you get to the 10-minute mark and can hear he's slowing down, it's worth waiting another minute.
- At ALL times, watch your baby on the video monitor to make sure he's safe.
- The 10-minute rule is the BACKBONE of this program. The 10-minute rule is going to teach your baby how to self-settle and at the end of the day, sleep through the night. You'll find that the time between wakeups will extend and the time it takes him to settle will shorten. One night, he'll only have one feed or sleep through the night. ☺

Night 4 to 6:
- ♥ Move your chair mid-room to reduce interaction. NO TOUCHING.

Night 7 to 9:
- ♥ Move your chair to the door or further away from him.

Night 10:
- ♥ Don't sit anywhere anymore. Put him down and walk out.
- ♥ Wait 10 minutes of crying, go back into the room, say your key phrase, some careful touch and leave again.
- ♥ If he gets really worked up, you can pick him up, walk around the room until he's calm. DON'T rock him with your legs while you, put him down again and walk out. **No Rocking**. Do all this until he falls asleep.

Nap Routine:

A very short but consistent nap routine is very important. Do the same thing every single time before a nap. Have the nap routine in your baby's room. Remember, there is no feed in a nap routine. You're going to feed your baby AFTER the sleep. If it happens that your baby needs a feed before the nap because it's the 3-hour mark, feed your baby a bit earlier and outside the room.

- ♥ Tell him it's nap time
- ♥ Walk him to his room
- ♥ Change his nappy

Newborn (0 to 4.5 months)

- ♥ Swaddle
- ♥ Cot (awake)

Nap
(Day 1 to 3):

- ♥ Sit beside the cot.
- ♥ Say repetitive key phrases.
- ♥ You can occasionally touch him on the shoulder **(for 3 seconds ONLY and then lift your hand up. Don't leave your hand on his body).** We don't want this to become a new external strategy he uses to fall asleep. Remember, it isn't your job to put him to sleep; you're only there to offer some comfort. It must be his job now to put himself to sleep.
- ♥ If he gets really worked up, you can pick him up and walk around the room until he's calm. NO ROCKING.
- ♥ **Try for 45 minutes**, if he hasn't slept, take a **15-minute break.** (Take him out of the cot, out of the room, have some quiet play)
- ♥ After the break, go back and try for another **30 minutes.**
- ♥ After 30 minutes, proceed with a **NAP EMERGENCY (page 130).**

Day 4 to 6:

- ♥ Move your chair mid-room to reduce interaction. NO TOUCHING.

Day 7 to 9:
- ♥ Move your chair to the door, or further away from him

Day 10:
- ♥ Don't sit anywhere anymore. Put him down and walk out.
- ♥ Wait 10 minutes of full crying, go back into the room, say your key phrase, some careful touch and leave again.
- ♥ If he gets really worked up, you can pick him up, walk around the room until he's calm, put him down again and walk out. **No rocking**. Do all this until he falls asleep.

The ideal situation is to do the "Camp Out" method during the day but if there is another sibling in the house or you have twins and you're on your own, unfortunately the "Camp Out" method isn't possible because your other child can't be left alone. In these situations, unfortunately, you'll have to do "Responsive Settling" from Day 1 which means you jump to Day 10 on this program.

Nap Emergency:

Babies must nap, they can't skip a nap because then they'll become overtired. This means they'll get worked up instead of down and then it gets VERY difficult to get them down to sleep. They almost look like hyperactive babies.

Newborn (0 to 4.5 months)

This is how nap emergency works:

You've tried to get your baby to sleep for 45 minutes with no success. You took a 15-minute break. After the break, you tried for another 30 minutes with no success. Now, you can proceed with a NAP EMERGENCY (you've tried for 1 hour and 30 minutes with no success). Now, you can do whatever worked before, such as:

- Take him for a walk in the pram
- Take him for a car ride
- Rock or pat him to sleep
- Bounce him
- Walk him to sleep in your arms
- Cuddle him in your arms
- Lay down with him.

The 2 things you're NOT allowed to do:

- NO FEEDING TO SLEEP!
- NO DUMMY!

He must sleep, we want to break the circle of overtiredness. The nap routine can be difficult initially, but it does follow through.

Another situation where we use nap emergency is with the LAST NAP of the day:

We use nap emergency at the end of the day if you need to fit in another catnap. You don't have time to try for 1 hour and 30 minutes to get your baby to sleep.

Happy Sleepers

This is how it works:

- You put him down in his cot for 10 minutes
- He doesn't fall asleep within 10 minutes
- Pick him up and do a nap emergency
- Only allow him to sleep for 20 minutes
- Wake him up and count his awake time to bedtime. (It might be after 9 pm)

<u>Example:</u>
Napped from 5 pm to 6:30 pm
Awake from 6:30 pm to 7:30 pm
Nap at 7:30 pm (your baby must be awake at 8 pm for a 9 pm bedtime).
At 7:30 pm, put your baby down for a nap. If he isn't asleep by 7:40 pm, pick him up and do nap emergency. Say it takes him 15 minutes to fall asleep (7:55 pm), let him sleep until 8:15 pm (20-minute nap). Bedtime will be at 9:15 pm.

<u>Another example:</u>
Napped from 4:30 pm to 6 pm
Awake from 6 pm to 7 pm
Nap at 7 pm (your baby must be awake at 8 pm for a 9 pm bedtime, you don't have 1 hour and 30 minutes to get him to sleep).
At 7:00 pm, put your baby down for a nap. If he isn't asleep by 7:10 pm, pick him up and do nap emergency. Say it takes him 15 minutes to fall asleep (7:25 pm), let him sleep until 8:00 pm (35 min nap). Bedtime will be at 9:00 pm.

Newborn (0 to 4.5 months)

Short Naps:

<u>If your baby only slept for 10 minutes to 1 hour and 20 minutes:</u>
- Wait 5 to 10 minutes of full crying.
- If he's still crying after 5 to 10 minutes, go in, turn him on his side and pat him on his bottom. Try to pat him back to sleep.
- Only keep on patting if it looks like he might go back to sleep for 15 – 20 minutes. **but if he keeps on crying after 1 minute of patting—stop and pick him**

<u>If your baby only slept for 1 hour and 20 minutes to 1 hour and 40 minutes:</u>
- ♥ Wait 5 to 10 minutes of full crying.
- ♥ If he's still crying after 5 to 10 minutes, pick him up.

<u>If your baby slept for more than 1 hour and 40 minutes:</u>
- ♥ Just pick him up, no waiting—he slept enough.

Summary:

Awake Time:

Please read Page 95 again about awake times

Newborn (0 to 4.5 months)

Daytime Routine:

<u>0 to 4 months (8 am to 9 pm) and 3 hourly feeds</u>
8:00 am – Wake
8:15 am – Milk feed (8 am, 11 am, 2 pm, 5 pm, 8 pm, top-up at 8:45 pm)
8:45 am – Nap
Your baby must be awake from 8:00 pm
8:30 pm – Start his bedtime routine
9:00 pm – Bedtime

<u>From 4 months (7 am to 7 pm) and 4 hourly feeds</u>
7:00 am – Wake
7:15 am – Milk feed + solids (7 am, 11 am, 3 pm, 7 pm)
9:00/9:30 am – Nap
Your baby must be awake at 5:00 pm for a 7 pm bedtime
6:30 pm – Start his bedtime routine
7:00 pm – Bedtime

Bedtime Routine:

<u>0 to 4 months:</u>
8:30 pm – Bath
Dress in pyjamas
Milk feed + sing (keep your baby wide awake)
Swaddle
9:00 pm – Cot (awake)

<u>4 to 4.5 months:</u>
6:30 pm – Bath
Dress in pyjamas
Milk feed + story (keep your baby wide awake)
Swaddle/sleeping bag
7:00 pm – Cot (awake)

Bedtime:
Talk, touch, only pick up if needed

Overnight:
<u>**9 pm to 12 am:**</u>
Wait 10 minutes of full crying
Settle your baby
NO feeding

<u>**12 am and after (3 hourly feeds):**</u>
Wait 10 minutes of full crying
Change nappy
Milk feed **(keep fully awake)**
Put your baby back down in the cot **(fully awake)**

Nap Routine:

- ♥ Tell him it's nap time
- ♥ Walk him to his room
- ♥ Change his nappy
- ♥ Swaddle
- ♥ Cot (awake)

Newborn (0 to 4.5 months)

Naptime:

- Talk, touch, only pick up if needed.
- Try for 45 minutes, 15-minute break, try for another 30 minutes, NAP EMERGENCY.

Short naps:

Nap: 10 minutes to 1 hour and 20 minutes:
- Wait 5 to 10 minutes of full crying.
- Pat for 10 to 20 minutes (if he keeps on crying after 1 minute of patting—stop and pick him up).
- Pick up, nap done if he isn't back to sleep.

Nap: 1 hour and 20 minutes to 1 hour and 40 minutes:
- Wait 5 to 10 minutes of full crying.
- If he's still crying after 5 to 10 minutes, pick him up.

Nap: More than 1 hour 40 min:
Just pick him up, no waiting—he slept enough.

Infants (4.5 months to 7 months)

Introduction:

The difference between a newborn and a baby between 4.5 to 7 months is:

- Longer awake times (2 – 3 hours)
- No pickup
- 4- hourly milk feeds instead of 3- hourly
- You can start solids
- Sleeping bag instead of swaddle
- Baby will be moving from 4 naps to 3 naps a day

The awake time for a 4.5 month to 7-month-old baby is a lot longer, which means there will be fewer naps. Usually from about 6.5 months, babies start skipping the third nap and they only have 2 naps during the day which makes structure and routine a lot easier.

Infants (4.5 months to 7 months)

We do pick up newborns when they cry but from 4.5 months, **we don't**. It's too stimulating Every single time you pick your baby up, you can add 5 – 15 minutes to his settling time. Please don't pick your baby up from 4.5 months once he's in the cot to sleep. Because you're not picking him up, please make sure the following is done:

- Fully fed (not hungry at all)
- Fully awake (not drowsy)
- Nappy is dry
- Has pain relief on board if he's teething

If you've done all of these then you know he's perfect, and nothing is wrong. He's angry because you don't pick him up and rock him to sleep. He's ok.

The feeding times for a newborn are usually 8 am, 11 am, 2 pm, 5 pm, 8 pm and top-up at bedtime at 9 pm. For 4 months old and older, the feeding times are 7 am, 11 am, 3 pm and 7 pm (one feed less during the day but they're taking more milk at a time).

You can start with solids from 4 months old.

Awake Time:

4.5 Months - 7 Months

Awake time BETWEEN NAPS

2 Hours - 3 Hours

Please read Page 95 again about awake times

Daytime Routine:

7:00 am – Wake
If your baby is still asleep at 7:00 am, please wake him. He needs structure and routine in his day. We also need 12 hours during the day to fit in all the naps and 4x feeds.

7:15 am – Milk feed + solids (30 minutes to an hour later) Milk feed every 4 hours (7 am, 11 am, 3 pm, 7 pm), If your baby is still asleep at the feeding time, please don't wake him for the feed. He'll wake himself when he's very hungry.

Infants (4.5 months to 7 months)

Approximately 9:00/9:30 am – Nap
Your baby needs 2 to 3 naps per day
1:00 pm – Lunch
2nd and 3rd Nap
Times depends on the length of the naps and awake times thereafter. You must work it out.
Your baby must be awake at 4 pm/4:30 pm for a 7 pm bedtime (depending on age and awake time)
5:30 pm – Dinner
6:30 pm – Start his bedtime routine
7:00 pm – Bedtime

I always recommend for the bedtime routine to be in the room where your baby is going to sleep. If you do the bedtime routine in the lounge or in your bedroom, once you're finished and walking to your baby's room to put him down for the night, it's almost like walking to **jail**. Anxiety builds up. More crying happens. There is no positive relationship with his nursery because your baby feels it's only a place where you dump him for sleep.

What we want is for your baby to have a positive relationship with his nursery. Once he has his bath, walk straight to the nursery, dress him in there, give him milk, read a story or sing a song (no playing), give attention. It's all positive and nice. Once your baby finishes the feed, put him in the sleeping bag and straight into the cot. No time for anxiety.

The bedtime routine should only be 30 minutes. Try not to extend it any longer. I know 30 minutes sounds very short but it's possible. If your baby takes a long time to drink, have a very short bath. As he gets better with the drinking, he can start having a longer bath.

> **6:30 pm** – Bath
> Dress in pyjamas
> Milk feed + story (keep your baby wide awake)
> Sleeping bag
> **7:00 pm** – Cot (awake)

<u>Reflux or "vomity" babies:</u>
If you've a reflux baby or a baby who is prone to vomiting, we usually swap the bath and the feed so there is more time for the milk to be digested.

> **6:30 pm** – Feed
> Bath
> Dress in pyjamas
> Story (keep your baby wide awake)
> Sleeping bag
> **7:00 pm** – Cot (awake)

Bedtime
(Night 1 to 3):

Let's start the process—good luck! You can do this! Remember, you're going to give your baby the GIFT OF SLEEP FOR THE REST OF HIS LIFE. Don't focus on the crying now. Don't allow the crying to run with your emotions. All babies cry. I have never worked with a baby who doesn't cry. It's VERY NORMAL. Your baby will resist the change.

Infants (4.5 months to 7 months)

Babies don't like change. They want things to stay the same, they don't know any better, but you do.

LET'S DO IT!

You've done your bedtime routine; your baby is in his cot, and he immediately starts crying. It's ok, your baby is fine. Walk across to the door, close it, and switch off the light.

- ♥ Sit beside the cot. Have some calming music in your ears to calm you down (earphones).
- ♥ Say repetitive key phrases ("Night-nighttime" or "It's sleepy time now").
- ♥ You can occasionally touch him on the shoulder **(for 3 seconds ONLY and then lift your hand up. Don't leave your hand on his body).** We don't want this to become a new external strategy he uses to fall asleep. Remember, it isn't your job to put him to sleep; you're only there to offer some comfort. It must be his job now to put himself to sleep.
- ♥ Do all this until he falls asleep. **No time limit.** (Babies at this age can easily cry for 45 - 90 minutes) ☹
- ♥ Once he's asleep, wait 5 minutes and then leave the room.

Overnight Waking and Feeding:

- ♥ <u>**7 pm to 11 pm:**</u> If your baby wakes between 7 pm and 11 pm you're going to **settle your baby**. NO FEEDING. You're only going to feed your baby 4 hourly overnight, not every time he wakes up.

Wait **10 minutes** of full-on crying (not whining or grizzling) before you respond to him at all. This will delay the gratification and prevent him from becoming more stimulated upon seeing you.
- If he's still protesting after 10 minutes, go in and repeat the same strategies you were using at bedtime. Stay with him and say your key phrases until he goes back to sleep. NO FEEDING.
- Repeat the same process each time he wakes before the 4 - hourly feeding mark.
- **<u>11 pm and after (4 - hourly feeds):</u>** We do 4 - hourly feeds overnight when your baby wakes himself. You don't have to wake your baby at the 4 hourly mark unless medically indicated. Wait **10 minutes** of full-on crying (not whining or grizzling) before you respond to him at all. You must wait the 10 minutes before the feed (even if you know he's hungry) because he might surprise you and go back to sleep. If he's still crying at the 10-minute mark, go in, pick him up, **change the nappy first.** This is to delay the gratification of the night time feeds. Your baby will be less likely to connect waking and crying with feeding.
- Keep an eye on him through the feed and do your best to **keep him awake**.
- He must go back to his cot awake.
- Please keep him in his room at night.
- Keep the lights low and your voice quiet.
- Night time is for sleeping, resist the urge to watch TV. This will also help you resettle faster when you get back to your own bed.

Infants (4.5 months to 7 months)

- ♥ Don't consider morning anything before 6:30 am. Make a big deal about it being morning and take him out of the bedroom for his first feed.

<u>The 10-minute rules:</u>
- He must cry full-on for 10 minutes. We don't count whining, grizzling, or blowing raspberries.
- If he cries for 4 minutes and he stops for more than 1 minute, you must restart the 10 minutes again.
- You must wait the full 10 minutes. A lot of babies cry for 9.5 minutes and then they resettle and go back to sleep for another 3 hours.
- If you get to the 10-minute mark and can hear he's slowing down, it's worth waiting another minute.
- At ALL times, watch your baby on the video monitor to make sure he's safe.
- The 10-minute rule is the BACKBONE of this program. The 10-minute rule is going to teach your baby how to self-settle and at the end of the day, sleep through the night. You'll find that the time between wakeups will extend and the time it takes him to settle will shorten. One night, he'll only have one feed or sleep through the night. ☺

<u>Night 4 to 6:</u>
- ♥ Move your chair mid-room to reduce interaction. NO TOUCHING.

<u>Night 7 to 9:</u>
- ♥ Move your chair to the door or further away from him.

Night 10:
- ♥ Don't sit anywhere anymore. Put him down and walk out.
- ♥ If he cries longer than 10 minutes, go back into the room, say your key phrase, some careful touch and leave again.
- ♥ Repeat every 10 minutes if necessary.
- ♥ Do all this until he falls asleep.

Nap Routine:

A very short but consistent nap routine is very important. Do the same thing every single time before a nap. Have the nap routine in your baby's room. Remember, there is no feed in a nap routine. You're going to feed your baby AFTER the sleep. If it happens that your baby needs a feed before the nap because it's the 4-hour mark, feed your baby a bit earlier and outside the room.

- ♥ Tell him it's nap time
- ♥ Walk him to his room
- ♥ Change his nappy
- ♥ Sleeping bag
- ♥ Cot (awake)

Nap
(Day 1 to 3):

- ♥ Sit beside the cot.

Infants (4.5 months to 7 months)

- Say repetitive key phrases.
- You can occasionally touch him on the shoulder **(for 3 seconds ONLY and then lift your hand up. Don't leave your hand on his body).** We don't want this to become a new external strategy he uses to fall asleep. Remember, it isn't your job to put him to sleep; you're only there to offer some comfort. It must be his job now to put himself to sleep.
- **Try for 1 hour.** If he hasn't slept, **take a 15-minute break.** (Take him out of the cot, out of the room, have some quiet play)
- After the break, go back and try for another **30 minutes.**
- After 30 minutes proceed with **NAP EMERGENCY (page 148).**

Day 4 to 6:
- Move your chair mid-room to reduce interaction. NO TOUCHING.

Day 7 to 9:
- Move your chair to the door, or further away from him.

Day 10:
- Don't sit anywhere anymore. Put him down and walk out.
- If he cries longer than 10 minutes, go back into the room, say your key phrase, some careful touch and leave again.
- Repeat every 10 minutes if necessary. Do all this until he falls asleep.

Nap Emergency:

Babies must nap, they can't skip a nap because then they'll become overtired. This means they'll get worked up instead of down and then it gets VERY difficult to get them down to sleep. They almost look like hyperactive babies.

This is how nap emergency works:

You've tried to get your baby to sleep for 1 hour with no success. You took a 15-minute break. After the break, you tried for another 30 minutes with no success. Now you can proceed with a NAP EMERGENCY (you've tried for 1 hour and 45 minutes with no success) and do whatever worked before:

- Take him for a walk in the pram
- Take him for a car ride
- Rock or pat him to sleep
- Bounce him
- Walk him to sleep in your arms
- Cuddle him in your arms
- Lay down with him

The 2 things you're NOT allowed to do:

- NO FEEDING TO SLEEP!
- NO DUMMY!

He must sleep, we want to break the circle of overtiredness. The nap routine can be difficult initially, but it does follow through.

Infants (4.5 months to 7 months)

Another situation where we use nap emergency is with the LAST NAP of the day:

We use a nap emergency at the end of the day if you need to fit in another catnap. You don't have time to try for 1 hour and 30 minutes to get your baby to sleep.

This is how it works:

- o You put him down in his cot for 10 minutes
- o He doesn't fall asleep within 10 minutes
- o Pick him up and do a nap emergency
- o Only allow him to sleep for 20 minutes
- o Wake him up and count his awake time to bedtime. (It might be after 7 pm)

<u>Example:</u>
Napped from 1:30 pm to 2:45 pm
Awake from 2:45 pm to 4:00 pm
Nap at 4:00 pm (your baby must be awake at 4:30 pm for a 7 pm bedtime)
At 4:00 pm, put your baby down for a nap. If he isn't asleep by 4:10 pm, pick him up and do nap emergency. Say it takes him 15 minutes to fall asleep (4:25 pm), let him sleep until 4:45 pm (20 min nap). Bedtime will be at 7:15 pm (a later bedtime is 100% fine).

<u>Another example:</u>
Napped from 1:00 pm to 2:15 pm
Awake from 2:15 pm to 3:30 pm
Nap at 3:30 pm (your baby must be awake at 4:30 pm for

> a 7 pm bedtime. You don't have 1 hour and 30 minutes to get him to sleep.)
>
> At 3:30 pm, put your baby down for a nap. If he isn't asleep by 3:40 pm, pick him up and do a nap emergency. Say it takes him 15 minutes to fall asleep (3:55 pm), let him sleep until 4:30 pm (35 min nap). Bedtime will be at 7:00 pm.

Short Naps:

If your baby only slept for 10 minutes to 1 hour and 20 minutes:
- ♥ Wait 10 minutes of full crying.
- ♥ If he's still crying after 5 to 10 minutes, go in, turn him on his side and pat him on his bottom. Try to pat him back to sleep.
- ♥ Only keep on patting if it looks like he might go back to sleep for 15 – 20 minutes. **But if he keeps on crying after 1 minute of patting—stop and pick him**

If your baby only slept for 1 hour and 20 minutes to 1 hour and 40 minutes:
- ♥ Wait 10 minutes of full crying.
- ♥ If he's still crying after 10 minutes, pick him up.

If your baby slept for more than 1 hour and 40 minutes:
- ♥ Just pick him up, no waiting—he slept enough.

Infants (4.5 months to 7 months)

Summary:

Awake Time:

Day Routine:

7:00 am – Wake
7:15 am – Milk feed + solids (30 minutes to an hour later) (7 am, 11 am, 3 pm, 7 pm)
Approximately 9:00/9:30 am – Nap
1:00 pm – Lunch
  Your baby must be awake at 4 pm/4:30 pm for a 7 pm bedtime (depending on age and awake time)
5:30 pm – Dinner
6:30 pm – Start his bedtime routine
7:00 pm – Bedtime

Bedtime Routine:

6:30 pm – Bath
Dress in pyjamas
Milk feed + story (keep your baby wide awake)
Sleeping bag
7:00 pm – Cot (awake)

Reflux babies:
6:30 pm – Feed
Bath
Dress in pyjamas
Story (keep your baby wide awake)
Sleeping bag
7:00 pm – Cot (awake)

Bedtime:

Talk and touch only

Overnight:

7 pm to 11 pm:
Wait 10 minutes of full crying
Settle your baby
NO feeding
11 pm and after (4 hourly feeds):
Wait 10 minutes of full crying
Change nappy

Infants (4.5 months to 7 months)

Milk feed **(keep fully awake)**
Put your baby back down in the cot **fully awake**

Nap Routine:

- Tell him it's nap time
- Walk him to his room
- Change his nappy
- Sleeping bag
- Cot (awake)
- Naptime

Naptime:

- Talk and touch.
- Try for 1 hour with a 15-minute break. Then, try for another 30 minutes. NAP EMERGENCY as a last resort.

Short Naps:

Nap: 10 minutes to 1 hour and 20 minutes:
- Wait 10 minutes of full crying.
- Pat for 10 to 20 minutes (if he keeps on crying after 1 minute of patting—stop and pick him up).
- Pick up, nap done if he isn't back to sleep.

Nap: 1 hour and 20 minutes to 1 hour and 40 minutes:
- Wait 10 minutes of full crying.
- If he's still crying after 10 minutes, pick him up.

Nap: More than 1 hour 40 min:
- Just pick him up, no waiting—he slept enough.

Infants (7 months – 13 months)

Introduction:

The difference between a 4.5-month to 7-month-old baby and 7-month to 13-month-old baby is:

- Longer awake times (3 – 4 hours)
- No overnight feeds
- Standing up
- Baby will be moving from 3 naps to 2 naps a day

From 7 months, babies don't need overnight feeds. They need uninterrupted sleep (11 to 12 hours) more than feeding. They'll start eating and drinking more during the day when you start skipping the feeds overnight.

Happy Sleepers

Usually from about 9 to 10 months, babies start standing up in the cot and parents don't know how to handle that. I will discuss this issue in this routine ☺

Awake Time:

7 Months - 13 Months

Awake time BETWEEN NAPS

3 Hours - 4 Hours

Please read Page 95 again about awake times

Daytime Routine:

7:00 am – Wake

If your baby is still asleep at 7:00 am, please wake him. He needs structure and routine in his day. We also need 12 hours during the day to fit in all the naps and 4x feeds.

Infants (7 months – 13 months)

7:15 am – Milk feed + solids
Milk feed every 4 hours (7 am, 11 am, 3 pm, 7 pm), If your baby is still asleep at the feeding time, please don't wake him for the feed. He'll wake himself if he's very hungry.

Approximately 9:30/9:45 am – Nap
Your baby needs 2 naps per day.

1:00 pm – Lunch

2nd Nap
Time depends on the length of the nap and awake times thereafter. You must work it out.
Your baby must be awake at 3:30 to 4 pm (depending on age and awake time).

5:30 pm – Dinner

6:30 pm – Start his bedtime routine

7:00 pm – Bedtime

I always recommend for the bedtime routine to be in the room where your baby is going to sleep. If you do the bedtime routine in the lounge or in your bedroom, once you're finished and walking to your baby's room to put him down for the night, it's almost like walking to **jail**. Anxiety builds up. More crying happens. There is no positive relationship with his nursery because your baby feels it's only a place where you dump him for sleep.

What we want is for your baby to have a positive relationship with his nursery. Once he has his bath, walk straight to the nursery, dress him in there, give him milk, read a story or sing a song (no playing), give attention. It's all positive and nice. Once your baby finishes the feed, put him in the sleeping bag and straight into the cot. No time for anxiety.

The bedtime routine should only be **30 minutes**. Try not to extend it any longer. I know 30 minutes sounds very short but it's possible. If your baby takes a long time to drink, have a very short bath. As he gets better with the drinking, he can start having a longer bath.

> **6:30 pm** – Bath
> Dress in pyjamas
> Milk feed + story (keep your baby wide awake)
> Sleeping bag
> **7:00 pm** – Cot (awake)

Reflux or "vomity" babies:
If you've a reflux baby or a baby who is prone to vomiting, we usually swap the bath and the feed so there is more time for the milk to be digested.

> **6:30 pm** – Feed
> Bath
> Dress in pyjamas
> Story (keep your baby wide awake)
> Sleeping bag
> **7:00 pm** – Cot (awake)

Bedtime
Night 1 to 3:

Let's start the process—good luck! You can do this! Remember, you're going to give your baby the GIFT OF SLEEP FOR THE REST OF HIS LIFE. Don't focus on the

Infants (7 months – 13 months)

crying now, don't allow the crying to run with your emotions. All babies cry. I have never worked with a baby who doesn't cry. It's VERY NORMAL. Your baby will resist the change. Babies don't like change. They want things to stay the same, they don't know any better, but you do.

LET'S DO IT!

You've done your bedtime routine, your baby is in his cot and he immediately starts crying. It's ok, your baby is fine. Walk across to the door, close it, and switch off the light.

- Sit beside the cot. Have some calming music in your ears to calm you down (earphones).
- Say repetitive key phrases ("Night-night time" or "It's sleepy time now").
- You can occasionally touch him on the shoulder **(for 3 seconds ONLY and then lift your hand up. Don't leave your hand on his body).** We don't want this to become a new external strategy he uses to fall asleep. Remember, it isn't your job to put him to sleep; you're only there to offer some comfort. It must be his job now to put himself to sleep.
- If he can stand up, try to lay him down 5 times only (10 minutes apart), then let him stand.
- Do all this until he falls asleep. **No time limit**. (Babies at this age can easily cry for 45 min to 90 min ☹).
- Once he's asleep, wait 5 minutes and then leave the room.

Overnight Waking:

When your baby wakes up, you're going to settle your baby the same way you did at bedtime. You're only going to sit there to support him in his learning, you're NOT there to help him.

- ♥ Wait 10 minutes (full-on crying, no whining or grizzling) before you respond to him at all.
- ♥ This will delay the gratification and prevent him from becoming more stimulated upon seeing you.
- ♥ If he's still protesting after 10 minutes, then go in and repeat the same strategies you were using at bedtime. Stay with him and say your key phrases until he goes back to sleep.
- ♥ Repeat the same process each time he wakes in the night.
- ♥ No night feedings.
- ♥ Don't consider morning anything before 6:30 am.
- ♥ Make a big deal about it being morning and take him out of the bedroom for his first feed.

<u>The 10-minute rules:</u>
- He must cry full-on for 10 minutes. We don't count whining, grizzling, or talking.
- If he cries for 4 minutes and he stops for more than 1 minute, you must restart the 10 minutes again.
- You must wait the full 10 minutes. A lot of babies cry for 9.5 minutes and then they resettle and go back to sleep for another 3 hours.
- If you get to the 10-minute mark and you can hear he's slowing down, it's worth waiting another minute.

Infants (7 months – 13 months)

- At ALL times, watch your baby on the video monitor to make sure he's safe.
- The 10-minute rule is the BACKBONE of this program. The 10-minute rule is going to teach your baby how to self-settle and, at the end of the day, sleep through the night. You'll find that the time between wakeups will extend and the time it takes him to settle will shorten. Then one night, he'll just start sleeping through the night. ☺

Night 4 to 6:
- Move your chair mid-room to reduce interaction. NO TOUCHING.

Night 7 to 9:
- Move your chair to the door or further away from him.

Night 10:
- Don't sit anywhere anymore. Put him down and walk out.
- If he cries longer than 10 minutes, go back into the room, say your key phrase, some careful touch and leave again.
- Repeat every 10 minutes if necessary.
- Do all this until he falls asleep.

Nap Routine:

- ♥ Tell him it's nap time
- ♥ Walk him to his room
- ♥ Change his nappy
- ♥ Sleeping bag
- ♥ Cot (awake)

Nap
(Day 1 to 3):
- ♥ Sit beside the cot.
- ♥ Say repetitive key phrases.
- ♥ If he stands up, try to lay him down 5 times only (10 minutes apart). Then, let him stand.
- ♥ You can occasionally touch him on the shoulder **(for 3 seconds ONLY and then lift your hand up. Don't leave your hand on his body).** We don't want this to become a new external strategy he uses to fall asleep. Remember, it isn't your job to put him to sleep; you're only there to offer some comfort. It must be his job now to put himself to sleep.
- ♥ **Try for 1 hour**, if he hasn't slept, **take a 15-minute break.** (Take him out of the cot, out of the room, have some quiet play)
- ♥ After the break, go back and try for another **30 minutes.**
- ♥ After 30 minutes, proceed with **NAP EMERGENCY (page 163).**

Infants (7 months – 13 months)

Day 4 to 6:
- ♥ Move your chair mid-room to reduce interaction. NO TOUCHING.

Day 7 to 9:
- ♥ Move your chair to the door, or further away from him.

Day 10:
- ♥ Don't sit anywhere anymore. Put him down and walk out.
- ♥ If he cries longer than 10 minutes, go back into the room, say your key phrase, some careful touch and leave again.
- ♥ Repeat every 10 minutes if necessary. Do all this until he falls asleep.

Nap Emergency:

Babies must nap, they can't skip a nap because then they'll become overtired. This means they'll get worked up instead of down and then it gets VERY difficult to get them down to sleep. They almost look like hyperactive babies.

This is how nap emergency works:

You've tried to get your baby to sleep for 1 hour with no success. You took a 15-minute break. After the break, you tried for another 30 minutes with no success. Now, you can proceed with a NAP EMERGENCY (you've tried for 1 hour and 45 minutes with no success) and do whatever worked before:

Happy Sleepers

Take him for a walk in the pram

- Take him for a car ride
- Rock or pat him to sleep
- Bounce him
- Walk him to sleep in your arms
- Cuddle him in your arms
- Lay down with him

The 2 things you're NOT allowed to do:

- NO FEEDING TO SLEEP!
- NO DUMMY!

He must sleep, we want to break the circle of overtiredness. The nap routine can be difficult initially but it does follow through.

Another situation where we use nap emergency is with the LAST NAP of the day:

We use a nap emergency at the end of the day if you need to fit in another catnap. You don't have time to try for 1 hour and 30 minutes to get your baby to sleep.

This is how it works:

- You put him down in his cot for 10 minutes
- He doesn't fall asleep within 10 minutes
- Pick him up and do a nap emergency
- Only allow him to sleep for 20 minutes

Infants (7 months – 13 months)

o   Wake him up and count his awake time to bedtime. (It might be after 7 pm)

<u>Example:</u>
Napped from 12:30 pm to 1:45 pm
Awake from 1:45 pm to 3:00 pm
Nap at 3:00 pm (your baby must be awake at 3:30 pm for a 7 pm bedtime)
At 3:00 pm, put your baby down for a nap. If he isn't asleep by 3:10 pm, pick him up and do a nap emergency. Say it takes him 15 minutes to fall asleep (3:25 pm), let him sleep until 3:45 pm (20-minute nap). Bedtime will be at 7:15 pm (a later bedtime is 100% fine).

<u>Another example:</u>
Napped from 12:00 pm to 1:15 pm
Awake from 1:15 pm to 2:30 pm
Nap at 2:30 pm (your baby must be awake at 3:30 pm for a 7 pm bedtime. You don't have 1 hour and 30 minutes to get him to sleep)
At 2:30 pm, put your baby down for a nap. If he isn't asleep by 2:40 pm, pick him up and do a nap emergency. Say it takes him 15 minutes to fall asleep (2:55 pm), let him sleep until 3:30 pm (35-minute nap). Bedtime will be at 7:00 pm.

Short Naps:

<u>If your baby only slept for 10 minutes to 1 hour and 20 minutes:</u>
- ♥ Wait 10 minutes of full crying.

- ♥ If he's still crying after 10 minutes, go in, turn him on his side and pat him on his bottom. Try to pat him back to sleep.
- ♥ Only keep on patting if it looks like he might go back to sleep for 15 – 20 minutes. **If he keeps on crying after 1 minute of patting—stop and pick him**

<u>If your baby only slept for 1 hour and 20 minutes to 1 hour and 40 minutes:</u>
- ♥ Wait 10 minutes of full crying.
- ♥ If he's still crying after 10 minutes, pick him up.

<u>If your baby slept for more than 1 hour and 40 minutes:</u>
- ♥ Just pick him up, no waiting—he slept enough.

Infants (7 months – 13 months)

Summary:

Awake Time:

Day Routine:

7:00 am – Wake
7:15 am – Milk feed + solids (30 minutes to an hour later)
9:00/9:30 am – Nap
1:00 pm – Lunch
   Your baby must be awake at 3:30/4:00 pm (depending on age and awake time)
5:30 pm – Dinner
6:30 pm – Start his bedtime routine
7:00 pm – Bedtime

Bedtime Routine:

6:30 pm – Bath
Dress in pyjamas
Milk feed + story (keep your baby wide awake)
Sleeping bag
7:00 pm – Cot (awake)

<u>Reflux or "vomity" babies:</u>
6:30 pm – Feed
Bath
Dress in pyjamas
Story (keep your baby wide awake)
Sleeping bag
7:00 pm – Cot (awake)

Bedtime:

Talk, touch and lay him down 5 times, 10 minutes apart if he can stand up.

Overnight:

Wait for 10 minutes of full crying
Settle your baby
NO feeding

Infants (7 months – 13 months)

Nap Routine:

- ♥ Tell him it's nap time
- ♥ Walk him to his room
- ♥ Change his nappy
- ♥ Sleeping bag
- ♥ Cot (awake)
- ♥ Naptime

Naptime:

Talk, touch and lay him down 5 times, 10 minutes apart if he can stand up.

Short Naps:

Nap: 10 minutes to 1 hour and 20 minutes:
- Wait 10 minutes of full crying.
- Pat for 10 to 20 minutes (if he keeps on crying after 1 minute of patting—stop and pick him up).
- Pick up, nap done if he isn't back to sleep.

Nap: 1 hour and 20 minutes to 1 hour and 40 minutes:
- Wait 10 minutes of full crying.
- If he's still crying after 10 minutes, pick him up.

Nap: More than 1 hour 40 min:
- Just pick him up, no waiting—he slept enough.

Infants (13 months to 19 months) - cot

Introduction:

The difference between a 7-month to 13-month-old baby and 13-months to 3-years is:

- Longer awake time (4 -5 hours)
- Baby will be moving from 2 naps to 1 nap
- Moving from 4 hourly milk feeds (4 feeds a day) to 2-3 milk feeds a day
- Giving solids first in the morning then milk

Infants (13 months to 19 months) - cot

Awake Time:

Please read Page 95 again about awake times

Daytime routine:

7:00 am – Wake
If your baby is still asleep at 7:00 am, please wake him. He needs structure and routine in his day. We also need 12 hours during the day to fit in all the naps and all his food.

7:30 am – Breakfast + milk
Solids are becoming a bit more important than milk. Always give solids first in the morning and milk 30 min – 60 min after. We don't want your baby to fill himself with milk and then don't want to eat the solids.

9:30 am - Snack
11:00 am - Lunch
Approximately 11:30/12 pm – Nap (Depending on his awake time)
Your baby must be awake at 1:30/2:00 pm (depending on age and awake time)
3:00 pm – Snack
5:30 pm – Dinner
6:30 pm – Start his bedtime routine
7:00 pm – Bedtime

I always recommend for the bedtime routine to be in the room where your baby is going to sleep. If you do the bedtime routine in the lounge or in your bedroom, once you're finished and walking to your baby's room to put him down for the night, it's almost like walking to **jail**. Anxiety builds up. More crying happens. There is no positive relationship with his nursery because your baby feels it's only a place where you dump him for sleep.

What we want is for your baby to have a positive relationship with his nursery. Once he has his bath, walk straight to the nursery, dress him in there, give him milk, read a story or sing a song (no playing), give attention. It's all positive and nice. Once your baby finishes the feed, put him in the sleeping bag and straight into the cot. No time for anxiety.

The bedtime routine should only be **30 minutes**. Try not to extend it any longer. I know 30 minutes sounds very short but it's possible. If your baby takes a long time to drink, have a very short bath. As he gets better with the drinking, he can start having a longer bath.

Infants (13 months to 19 months) - cot

6:30 pm – Bath
Dress in pyjamas
Milk feed + story (keep your baby wide awake)
Sleeping bag
7:00 pm – Cot (awake)

Bedtime
(Night 1 to 3):

Let's start the process—good luck! You can do this! Remember, you're going to give your baby the GIFT OF SLEEP FOR THE REST OF HIS LIFE. Don't focus on the crying now, don't allow the crying to run with your emotions. All babies cry. I have never worked with a baby who doesn't cry. It's VERY NORMAL. Your baby will resist the change. Babies don't like change. They want things to stay the same, they don't know any better, but you do.

LET'S DO IT!

You've done your bedtime routine, your baby is in his cot and he immediately starts crying. It's ok, your baby is fine. Walk across to the door, close it, and switch off the light.

- Sit beside the cot. Have some calming music in your ears to calm you down (earphones).
- Say repetitive key phrases ("Night-night time" or "It's sleepy time now").
- You can occasionally touch him on the shoulder **(for 3 seconds ONLY and then lift your hand up. Don't**

leave your hand on his body). We don't want this to become a new external strategy he uses to fall asleep. Remember, it isn't your job to put him to sleep; you're only there to offer some comfort. It must be his job now to put himself to sleep.

- If he can stand up, try to lay him down 5 times only (10 minutes apart), then let him stand.
- Do all this until he falls asleep. **No time limit** (Babies at this age can easily cry for 45 to 90 minutes ☹).
- Once he's asleep, wait 5 minutes, then leave the room.

Overnight Waking (no feeding):

When your baby wakes up, you're going to settle your baby the same way you did at bedtime. You're only going to sit there to support him in his learning, you're NOT there to help him.

- ♥ Wait 10 minutes (full-on crying, no whining or grizzling) before you respond to him at all.
- ♥ This will delay the gratification and prevent him from becoming more stimulated upon seeing you.
- ♥ If he's still protesting after 10 minutes, go in and repeat the same strategies you were using at bedtime. Stay with him and say your key phrases until he goes back to sleep.
- ♥ Repeat the same process each time he wakes in the night.
- ♥ No night feedings.
- ♥ Don't consider morning anything before 6:30 am.

Infants (13 months to 19 months) - cot

- ♥ Make a big deal about it being morning and take him out of the bedroom for his breakfast.

The 10-minute rules:
- He must cry full-on for 10 minutes, we don't count whining, grizzling, or talking.
- If he cries for 4 minutes and he stops for more than 1 minute, you must restart the 10 minutes again.
- You must wait the full 10 minutes. A lot of babies cry for 9.5 minutes and then they resettle and go back to sleep for another 3 hours.
- If you get to the 10-minute mark and you can hear he's slowing down, it's worth waiting another minute.
- At ALL times, watch your baby on the video monitor to make sure he's safe.
- The 10-minute rule is the BACKBONE of this program. The 10-minute rule is going to teach your baby how to self-settle and, at the end of the day, sleep through the night. You'll find that the time between wake-ups will extend and the time it takes him to settle will shorten. Then 1 night, he'll just start sleeping through the night. ☺

Night 4 to 6:
- ♥ Move your chair mid-room to reduce interaction. NO TOUCHING.

Night 7 to 9:
- ♥ Move your chair to the door or further away from him.

Night 10:
- ♥ Don't sit anywhere anymore. Put him down and walk out.
- ♥ If he cries for longer than 10 minutes, go back into the room, say your key phrase, some careful touch and leave again.
- ♥ Repeat every 10 minutes if necessary.
- ♥ Do all this until he falls asleep.

Nap Routine:

- ♥ Tell him it's nap time
- ♥ Walk him to his room
- ♥ Change his nappy
- ♥ Sleeping bag
- ♥ Cot (awake)

Nap
(Day 1 to 3):
- ♥ Sit beside the cot.
- ♥ Say repetitive key phrases.
- ♥ If he stands up, try to lay him down 5 times only (10 minutes apart). Then, let him stand.
- ♥ You can occasionally touch him **(for 3 seconds ONLY, then lift your hand up. Don't leave your hand on his body).** Be cautious that this doesn't become a new external strategy he uses to fall asleep. Remember, it isn't your job to put him to sleep; you're only there

to offer some comfort. It must be his job now to put himself to sleep.
- ♥ **Try for 1 hour**, then proceed with **a NAP EMERGENCY (next section).**

Day 4 to 6:
- ♥ Move your chair mid-room to reduce interaction. NO TOUCHING.

Day 7 to 9:
- ♥ Move your chair to the door, or further away from him.

Day 10:
- ♥ Don't sit anywhere anymore. Put him down and walk out.
- ♥ If he cries longer than 10 minutes, go back into the room, say your key phrase, some careful touch and leave again.
- ♥ Repeat every 10 minutes if necessary. Do all this until he falls asleep.

Nap Emergency:

Babies must nap, they can't skip a nap because then they'll become overtired, which means they'll get worked up instead of down. Then, it gets VERY difficult to get them to sleep. They almost look like hyperactive babies.

This is how a nap emergency works:

You've tried to get your baby to sleep for 1 hour with no success. Now, you can proceed with a NAP EMERGENCY and do whatever worked before:

- Take him for a walk in the pram
- Take him for a car ride
- Rock or pat him to sleep
- Bounce him
- Walk him to sleep in your arms
- Cuddle him in your arms
- Lay down with him.

The 2 things you're NOT allowed to do:

- NO FEEDING TO SLEEP!
- NO DUMMY!

He must sleep, we want to break the circle of overtiredness. The nap routine can be difficult initially but it does follow through.

Short Naps:

<u>If your baby only slept for 10 minutes to 1 hour and 20 minutes:</u>
- ♥ Wait 10 minutes of full crying.
- ♥ If he's still crying after 10 minutes, go in, turn him on his side and pat him on his bottom. Try to pat him back to sleep.
- ♥ Only keep on patting if it looks like he might go back to sleep for 15 – 20 minutes. **If he keeps on crying after 1 minute of patting—stop and pick him**

Infants (13 months to 19 months) - cot

<u>If your baby only slept for 1 hour and 20 minutes to 1 hour and 40 minutes:</u>
Wait 10 minutes of full crying.

- ♥ If he's still crying after 10 minutes, pick him up.

<u>If your baby slept for more than 1 hour and 40 minutes:</u>
- ♥ Just pick him up, no waiting—he slept enough.

Summary:

Awake Time:

Day Routine:

7:00 am – Wake
7:30 am – Breakfast + milk (half an hour to an hour later)
9:30 am - Snack
11:00 am - Lunch
12:00 pm – Nap
   Your baby must be awake at 1:30/2:00 pm (depending on age and awake time)
3:00 pm – Snack
5:30 pm – Dinner

Infants (13 months to 19 months) - cot

6:30 pm – Start his bedtime routine
7:00 pm – Bedtime

Bedtime Routine:

6:30 pm – Bath
Dress in pyjamas
Milk feed + story (keep your baby wide awake)
Sleeping bag
7:00 pm – Cot (awake)

Reflux or "vomity" babies:
6:30 pm – Feed
Bath
Dress in pyjamas
Story (keep your baby wide awake)
Sleeping bag
7:00 pm – Cot (awake)

Bedtime:

Talk, touch and lay him down 5 times, 10 minutes apart if he can stand up.

Overnight:

Wait 10 minutes of full crying
Settle your baby
NO feeding

Nap Routine:

- ♥ Tell him it's nap time
- ♥ Walk him to his room
- ♥ Change his nappy
- ♥ Sleeping bag
- ♥ Cot (awake)
- ♥ Naptime

Naptime:

Talk, touch and lay him down 5 times, 10 minutes apart if he can stand up.

Short Naps:

Nap: 10 minutes to 1 hour and 20 minutes:
- Wait 10 minutes of full crying.
- Pat for 10 to 20 minutes (if he keeps on crying after a minute of patting, stop and pick him up).
- Pick up, nap done if he isn't back to sleep.

Nap: 10 minutes to 1 hour and 20 minutes:
- Wait 10 minutes of full crying.
- If he's still crying after 10 minutes, pick him up.

Nap: More than 1 hour and 40 minutes:
- Just pick him up, no waiting—he slept enough.

Toddlers (19 months to 4 years – Cot)

Introduction:

The difference between a 13-month to 19-month toddler and 19-months to 4-years is:

- Longer awake times (5 – 6 hours)
- Some toddlers start to skip naps from 2.5 years old
- If you sleep train your toddler at 19 months and older for the first time, it can be a bit more difficult in terms of crying because they've the energy and strength to persist. I have a different approach here.

Awake Time:

Please read Page 95 again about awake times

Toddlers (19 months to 4 years – Cot)

Daytime Routine:

Toddler with **1 nap:**
- **7:00 am –** Wake

  If your toddler is still asleep at 7:00 am, please wake him. He needs structure and routine in his day.
- **7:30 am –** Breakfast + milk

  Solids are more important than milk at this stage. Always give solids first in the morning and milk 30 min – 60 min after. We don't want your toddler to fill himself with milk and then don't want to eat the solids.
- **9:30 am –** Snack
- **11:00 am –** Lunch
- **Approximately 12/12:30 pm –** Nap (Depends on his awake time)

  Your toddler must be awake at 1:30/2:00 pm (depending on age and awake time)
- **3:00 pm –** Snack
- **5:30 pm –** Dinner
- **6:30 pm –** Start his bedtime routine
- **7:00 pm –** Bedtime

Toddler with **no nap:**
- **7:00 am –** Wake

  If your toddler is still asleep at 7:00 am, please wake him. He needs structure and routine in his day.
- **7:30 am –** Breakfast
- **11:00 am –** Lunch
- **12:00 to 1 pm – Rest time (no nap) –** NO ACTIVE PLAY
- **3:00 pm –** Snack
- **5:30 pm –** Dinner

6:30 pm – Start his bedtime routine
7:00 pm – Bedtime

Bedtime Routine:

I always recommend for the bedtime routine to be in the room where your toddler is going to sleep. If you do the bedtime routine in the lounge or in your bedroom, once you're finished and walking to your toddler's room to put him down for the night, it's almost like walking to **jail**. Anxiety builds up. More crying happens. There is no positive relationship with his bedroom because your toddler feels it's only a place where you dump him for sleep.

What we want is for your toddler to have a positive relationship with his bedroom. Once he has his bath, walk straight to the bedroom, dress him in there, give him milk, read a story, or sing a song (no playing), give attention. It's all positive and nice. Once your toddler finishes the feed, put him in the sleeping bag and straight into the cot. No time for anxiety.

The bedtime routine should only be **30 minutes**. Try not to extend it any longer. I know 30 minutes sounds very short, but it's possible. If your toddler takes a long time to drink his milk, have a very short bath. As he gets better with the drinking, he can start having a longer bath.

6:30 pm – Bath
Dress in pyjamas
Milk feed + story (keep your toddler wide awake)

Toddlers (19 months to 4 years – Cot)

Sleeping bag
7:00 pm – Cot (awake)

Bedtime
(Night 1 to 3):

Let's start the process—good luck! You can do this! Remember, you're going to give your toddler the GIFT OF SLEEP FOR THE REST OF HIS LIFE. Don't focus on the crying now, don't allow the crying to run with your emotions. All babies and toddler's cry. I have never worked with a baby or toddler who doesn't cry. It's VERY NORMAL. Your toddler will resist the change. Toddlers don't like change. They want things to stay the same, they don't know any better, but you do.

LET'S DO IT!

You've done your bedtime routine, your toddler is in his cot and he immediately starts crying. It's ok, your toddler is fine. Walk across to the door, close it, and switch off the light.

- ♥ Sit beside the cot. Have some calming music in your ears to calm you down (earphones).
- ♥ Say repetitive key phrases ("Night-night time" or "It's sleepy time now").
- ♥ You can occasionally touch him on the shoulder **(for 3 seconds ONLY and then lift your hand up. Don't leave your hand on his body).** We don't want this to become a new external strategy he uses to fall asleep.

Remember, it isn't your job to put him to sleep; you're only there to offer some comfort. It must be his job now to put himself to sleep.

- ♥ If he can stand up, try to lay him down 5 times only, then let him stand.
- ♥ Do all this until he falls asleep. **No time limit**. (Toddler's at this age can easily cry for 45 to 90 minutes ☹).
- ♥ Once he's asleep, wait 5 minutes, then leave the room.

EXTREME MEASURE ONE (After 1 hour and 45 minutes and he's still screaming):

If your toddler is still crying after 1 hour and 45 min there can be a few reasons:

- You picked up your child a few times and you were not meant to. The pickups are VERY stimulating, and it WILL extend the settling time. Please STOP picking up your child.
- Your child is teething, and you didn't give him something for pain or what you gave isn't enough. Please give more.
- Your child might be too hot or cold, please check. Touch his face not his hands or feet.
- There is too much stimulation or distraction in the room
- The room isn't dark enough
- You have a very strong-willed child, it's ok. Just keep going.
- What we're doing isn't working for him, we need a different approach.

Toddlers (19 months to 4 years – Cot)

We must change what we're doing:

- ♥ If he keeps screaming, give him only one warning— no touching (After 1 hour and 45 minutes).
- ♥ Tell him: "If you're not going to stop screaming, lay down and try to go to sleep, Mummy is going to leave the room and lock the door."
- ♥ If he decides to keep on screaming, stand up, walk out, and close the door for **only 1 minute.**
- ♥ He will get upset.
- ♥ After 1 minute, go back into the room and sit in the chair. Say again: "It's sleepy time now, lay down and go to sleep. If you don't Mummy will walk out and lock the door again"
- ♥ If he decides not to listen, walk out again but this time, close the door for **2 minutes.** If he does listen, praise him immediately. "Thank you, Michael, for listening to Mummy. Mummy is so proud of you." – See Consequences and Rewards section (page 201)
- ♥ Repeat the process but increase the time between each step up to 5 minutes.

If your child doesn't get that upset when you leave the room, you might get something else to upset him. I know this sounds horrible but to change behaviour you have to upset him enough he doesn't want to do it again. Once he responds then you reward him. By removing a comforter might also work. See the consequences and rewards section on page 201.

EXTREME MEASURE 2 (After you've extended your time out of the room to 5 minutes):

You've done 5 minutes out of the room and your child is still crying and not asleep. Your presence in the room is distracting him, you must leave the room.

- ♥ If your toddler is still screaming, leave the room for 10 minutes.
- ♥ Go back into the room, check if he's ok and leave again for another 10 minutes.
- ♥ Go back into the room, check if he's ok and leave again—this time for 15 minutes.
- ♥ Repeat the process and increase the time by 5 minutes until he sleeps (20 minutes, 25 minutes, 30 minutes).
  (Some toddlers can be very strong and stubborn and refuse to give up their habits. **Please** try to be strong.) We're also open negotiation with your child ☺. If he screams and say: "I will lay down and stop but please sit down and don't leave the room", you can do that but the minute he starts again, you get up and leave for 10 minutes.

Overnight Waking:

When your baby wakes up, you're going to settle your baby the same way you did at bedtime. You're only going to sit there to support him in his learning, you're NOT there to help him.

Toddlers (19 months to 4 years – Cot)

- ♥ Wait for 10 to 15 minutes (full-on crying—not whining or grizzling) before you respond to him at all.
- ♥ This will delay the gratification and prevent him from becoming more stimulated upon seeing you.
- ♥ If he's still protesting after 10 to 15 minutes, go in and repeat the same strategies you were using at bedtime. Stay with him and say your key phrases until he goes back to sleep.
- ♥ Repeat the same process each time he wakes in the night.
- ♥ No night feedings.
- ♥ Don't consider morning anything before 6:30 am.
- ♥ Make a big deal about it being morning and take him out of the bedroom for breakfast.

The 10-minute rules:
- He must cry full-on for 10 minutes. We don't count whining, grizzling, or talking.
- If he cries for 4 minutes and he stops for more than a minute, you must restart the 10 minutes again.
- You must wait the full 10 minutes. A lot of babies cry for 9.5 minutes and then they resettle and go back to sleep for another 3 hours.
- If you get to the 10-minute mark and you can hear he's slowing down, it's worth waiting another minute.
- At ALL times, watch your baby on the video monitor to make sure he's safe.
- The 10-minute rule is the BACKBONE of this program. The 10-minute rule is going to teach your toddler how to self-settle and at the end of the day, sleep through the night. You'll find that the time between wake-ups

will extend and the time it takes him to settle will shorten. Then 1 night, he'll just start sleeping through the night. ☺

Night 4 to 6:
- ♥ Move your chair mid-room to reduce interaction. NO TOUCHING.

Night 7 to 9:
- ♥ Move your chair to the door or further away from him.

Night 10:
- ♥ Don't sit anywhere anymore. Put him down and walk out.
- ♥ If he cries for longer than 10 minutes, go back into the room, say your key phrase, some careful touch and leave again.
- ♥ Repeat every 10 minutes if necessary.
- ♥ Do all this until he falls asleep.

Nap Routine:

- ♥ Tell him it's nap time
- ♥ Walk him to his room
- ♥ Change his nappy
- ♥ Sleeping bag
- ♥ Cot (awake)

Toddlers (19 months to 4 years – Cot)

Nap

(Day 1 to 3):
- ♥ Sit beside the cot.
- ♥ Say repetitive key phrases.
- ♥ If he stands up, try to lay him down 5 times only (10 minutes apart). Then, let him stand.
- ♥ You can occasionally touch him **(for 3 seconds ONLY, then lift your hand up. Don't leave your hand on his body)**. Be cautious that this doesn't become a new external strategy he uses to fall asleep. Remember, it isn't your job to put him to sleep; you're only there to offer some comfort. It must be his job now to put himself to sleep.
- ♥ **Try for 45 minutes,** then proceed with **a NAP EMERGENCY** (page 194).

Day 4 to 6:
- ♥ Move your chair mid-room to reduce interaction. NO TOUCHING.

Day 7 to 9:
- ♥ Move your chair to the door, or further away from him.

Day 10:
- ♥ Don't sit anywhere anymore. Put him down and walk out.
- ♥ If he cries longer than 10 minutes, go back into the room, say your key phrase, some careful touch and leave again.
- ♥ Repeat every 10 minutes if necessary. Do all this until he falls asleep.

Nap Emergency:

Babies must nap, they can't skip a nap because then they'll become overtired. This means they'll get worked up instead of down. Then, it gets VERY difficult to get them to sleep. They almost look like hyperactive babies.

This is how a nap emergency works:

You've tried to get your baby to sleep for 45 minutes with no success. Now, you can proceed with a NAP EMERGENCY and do whatever worked before:

- Take him for a walk in the pram
- Take him for a car ride
- Rock or pat him to sleep
- Bounce him
- Walk him to sleep in your arms
- Cuddle him in your arms
- Lay down with him

The 2 things you're NOT allowed to do:

- NO FEEDING TO SLEEP!
- NO DUMMY!

He must sleep, we want to break the circle of overtiredness. The nap routine can be difficult initially but it does follow through.

Toddlers (19 months to 4 years – Cot)

Short naps:

At this age 1- hour to 1.5-hour nap is more than enough.

<u>If your baby only slept for 10 minutes to 1 hour and 20 minutes:</u>
- ♥ Wait 10 minutes of full crying
- ♥ If he's still crying after 10 minutes, pick him up.

Summary:

Awake Time:

Toddlers (19 months to 4 years – Cot)

Daytime Routine:

Toddler with **1 nap:**
    7:00 am – Wake
    7:30 am – Breakfast + milk
    9:30 am – Snack
    11:00 am – Lunch
    12:00 pm – Nap
    Your toddler must be awake at 1:30/2:00 pm (depending on age and awake time)
    3:00 pm – Snack
    5:30 pm – Dinner
    6:30 pm – Start his bedtime routine
    7:00 pm – Bedtime

Toddler with **no nap:**
    7:00 am – Wake
    7:30 am – Breakfast
    11:00 am - Lunch
    12:00 – 1:00 pm – Rest time (no nap) – NO ACTIVE PLAY
    3:00 pm – Snack
    5:30 pm – Dinner
    6:30 pm – Start his bedtime routine
    7:00 pm – Bedtime

Bedtime Routine:

    6:30 pm – Bath
    Dress in pyjamas
    Milk feed + story (keep your toddler wide awake)

Sleeping bag
7:00 pm – Cot (awake)

Bedtime:

Talk, touch and lay him down 5 times, 10 minutes apart if he can stand up.

After 1 hour and 45 minutes, proceed with Extreme Measure 1 and 2.

Overnight:

Wait 10 minutes of full crying
Settle your toddler
NO feeding

Nap Routine:

- ♥ Tell him it's nap time
- ♥ Walk him to his room
- ♥ Change his nappy
- ♥ Sleeping bag
- ♥ Cot (awake)

Toddlers (19 months to 4 years – Cot)

Naptime:

Talk, touch and lay him down 5 times, 10 minutes apart if he can stand up.

Short Naps:

Nap: 10 minutes to 1 hour and 20 minutes:
- Wait 10 minutes of full crying.
- If he's still crying after 10 minutes, pick him up.

Toddlers in a bed (>2.5 years – In a toddler bed)

Introduction:

Now we're going to talk about toddlers who are already in a toddler bed with no more naps. At Happy Sleepers, we never move a toddler out of his cot before the age of 2.5 years but if you can, closer to 3 years. Your toddler must understand the concept: "I'm in a big boy bed now and I'm not allowed to get out of my bed. If I do, there will be a consequence."

If he doesn't understand that, he isn't ready for a toddler bed. A lot of parents move their toddlers into a toddler bed prematurely. Yes, maybe in the beginning your toddler stays in the cot (honeymoon phase), and then after 1 month, he starts getting out. What are you going to start doing?

Toddlers in a bed (>2.5 years – In a toddler bed)

- Lay down next to him until he sleeps.
- Sit down next to him until he sleeps.
- Start holding his hand until he sleeps.
- Rubbing his back until he sleeps.

What is happening here? You as a parent become a sleep association or the rubbing, hand-holding, or patting becomes the sleep association. This situation gets harder and harder as they get older. Your child isn't ready for a toddler bed. Put him back into the cot.

Read page 226 "How to keep my toddler inside the cot"

Consequences, rewards, and constant requests:

I would like to talk about consequences and rewards when you work with a toddler who is already in a bed. When you sleep train a toddler in a bed, you're not only trying to improve the sleep, you also have to deal with the behaviour aspect. Toddlers, especially tired ones, can be very grumpy. This can lead you to a position where the child dictates whatever he wants, and you give in because you're so tired or you just can't be bothered. The problem then is that you get into a situation where you almost become the child and the child becomes the parent, which is a very dangerous place to be.

Boundaries are very important to make a child feel safe. When a child can do whatever they want, they can feel insecure, and massive behaviour problems, like temper tantrums, occur. It's very important for a parent to get their position as a parent back and we do this when we sleep train toddlers.

I do understand that you might have a very strong-willed child but even for that child, boundaries are important. That's why we have to talk about consequences and rewards because that's how we're going to manage the behaviour. A lot of parents find it very difficult to be firm with their toddlers, please practice in front of a mirror. Consistency with toddlers are VERY important, it's necessary to have one plan, structure, and routine. Decide one way how you're going to respond to your child to avoid both of you getting confused and overwhelmed. Your child must know, these are the rules and if he doesn't follow them, there will be an immediate consequence.

When parents want to change behaviour, they always start with a reward chart, and unfortunately, that doesn't work. You must use a consequence to change behaviour and when your child responds, you reward the positive behaviour. Toddlers usually love pleasing their parents, when you start rewarding and praising your child, he'll start loving the attention and want more of it.

<u>Let's start with rewards first.</u> A few examples of rewards are:

- Reward chart
- Praise ("Michael, you're Mummy's big boy. Mummy is so proud of you!")
- Food (ice cream for breakfast or he can choose breakfast)

Toddlers in a bed (>2.5 years – In a toddler bed)

- Get a basket with small gifts, keep it somewhere where he can see it for small achievements.
- Have a bigger gift for when he starts sleeping through the night.

Consequences:

At the bedtime routine, we can use the book as a consequence. Your toddler must sit up (no laying down) on your lap or the bed and listen to the story. If he walks around or doesn't want to sit still, you give him one warning. If he doesn't listen, then NO MORE STORY and put him straight into bed. The removal of the story is the consequence.

At bedtime or overnight, we usually use "locking the door" as a consequence, or you can remove a comforter. At Happy Sleepers, we use the "camp out" method to do the sleep training. The "camp out" method means you're sitting right next to your child until he falls asleep. He isn't allowed to talk to you, touch you, get out of bed, sit up or scream. The only thing he's allowed to do is lay down and cry if he wants to. If he does anything else, you give him a warning first and then you walk out. (This will be discussed in more detail in the Bedtime and Overnight section.)

When a child is stuck in a pitch-black room, by himself for 1 minute, they get VERY UPSET. Unfortunately, that's what you want because you want to stop the behaviour. When you walk back into the room, you tell him that you're happy to sit next to him until he falls asleep, but he must lay down and try to go to sleep. After 2 or 3 consequences, the child will usually say to sit in the chair, he will not get up again.

If he does what you say, praise him IMMEDIATELY. This is very important. "Thank you, Michael. Mummy is so proud of you for listening." The same goes for overnight. If he gets up, consequence him for getting up but sit next to him until he falls asleep.

With consequences at bedtime, overnight and during the day, it's very important to give a warning first and then follow through with a consequence IMMEDIATELY. You can't say: "When we get home, you will not be able to go onto the iPad." It must be immediate.

Constant requests:
With toddlers at bedtime, they can also have constant requests to drag out bedtime. Remember, a bedtime routine should only be 30 minutes (including the bath). They'll ask:

- Can I have some water?
- Can I have another cuddle?
- Can I go to the toilet again?
- Can I have another story or 4?
- Can I have another toy in my bed?

Don't offer it, but when your toddler starts with a request, tell him: "Michael, you only have one request. You can choose what you want, but once you chose, NO MORE." You have to follow through with NO MORE. Consistency with toddlers are VERY IMPORTANT!

Toddlers in a bed (>2.5 years – In a toddler bed)

Awake Time:

If your toddler doesn't need a nap, he still needs a 7:00 am to 7:00 pm schedule. He still needs 12 hours of awake time during the day with a **rest time** between 12 pm and 1 pm where no active play happens. In this time, your toddler can read a book, watch a movie, or play with Lego. He still needs the opportunity to sleep for 12 hours overnight.

Daytime routine:

Toddler with **1 nap**:
- **7:00 am – Wake**
  If your toddler is still asleep at 7:00 am, please wake him. He needs structure and routine in his day.
- **7:30 am** – Breakfast
- **9:30 am** – Snack
- **11:00 am** – Lunch
- **Approximately 12:30/12:45 pm** – Nap
  Your toddler must be awake at 1:30 pm (depending on age and awake time)
- **3:00 pm** – Snack
- **5:30 pm** – Dinner
- **6:30 pm** – Start his bedtime routine
- **7:00 pm** – Bedtime

Toddler with **no nap**:
- **7:00 am** – Wake
  If your toddler is still asleep at 7:00 am, please wake him. He needs structure and routine in his day.

7:30 am – Breakfast
11:00 am – Lunch
12:00 to 1 pm – Rest time (no nap) – NO ACTIVE PLAY
3:00 pm – Snack
5:30 pm – Dinner
6:30 pm – Start his bedtime routine
7:00 pm – Bedtime

I always recommend for the bedtime routine to be in the room where your toddler is going to sleep. If you do the bedtime routine in the lounge or in your bedroom, once you're finished and walking to your toddler's room to put him down for the night, it's almost like walking to **jail**. Anxiety builds up. More crying happens. There is no positive relationship with his bedroom because your toddler feels it's only a place where you dump him for sleep.

What we want is for your toddler is to have a positive relationship with his bedroom. Once he has his bath, walk straight to the bedroom, dress him, give him milk, read a story or sing a song (no playing), give attention. It's all positive and nice. Once your toddler finished his milk, put him straight into his bed. No time for anxiety. The bedtime routine should only be **30 minutes**. Try not to extend it any longer. I know 30 minutes sounds very short but it's possible.

With toddlers in a bed we also use a Toddler Gro Clock to show them when it's "sleepy time" (stay in your bed time) and when it's "wake up time" (you can get out of your bed). Show him the clock before you put him down.

Toddlers in a bed (>2.5 years – In a toddler bed)

6:30 pm – Bath
Dress in pyjamas
Story (keep your toddler wide awake)
Clock
7:00 pm – Bed (awake)

Bedtime
(Night 1 to 3):

- ♥ Sit beside the bed far enough away from him that he's unable to touch you.
- ♥ Show him the clock.
- ♥ Say repetitive key phrases ("Night-night time" or "It's sleepy time now").
- ♥ You can occasionally touch him on the shoulder. **(for 3 seconds ONLY and then lift your hand up. Don't leave your hand on his body).** We don't want this to become a new external strategy he uses to fall asleep. You're only there to offer some comfort. It must be his job now to put himself to sleep. YOU CAN TOUCH HIM, HE ISN'T ALLOWED TO TOUCH YOU!
- ♥ If he keeps screaming, sitting up, or trying to touch you, give him one warning.
- ♥ Tell him: "If you're not going to stop screaming, sitting up, or touching Mummy, Mummy is going to leave the room and lock the door."
- ♥ If he decides to keep screaming, sitting up, or touching Mummy, stand up, walk out and close the door for only 1 minute.
- ♥ He'll get upset.

- After 1 minute, go back into the room, refer to the clock and sit in the chair. Say again: "It's sleepy time now."
- If he decides to start screaming again, walk out again but this time, close the door for 2 minutes.
- Repeat the process but increase the minutes to a **maximum** of 5 minutes.

<u>EXTREME MEASURES</u> (After you've extended your time out of the room to 5 minutes):

- If your toddler is still screaming, leave the room for 10 minutes.
- Go back into the room, check if he's ok and leave again for another 10 minutes.
- Go back into the room, check if he's ok and leave again—this time for 15 minutes.
- Repeat the process and increase the time by 5 minutes until he sleeps (20 minutes, 25 minutes, 30 minutes). (Some toddlers can be very strong and stubborn and refuse to give up their habits. **Please** try to be strong)
- Do all this until he falls asleep. NO TIME LIMIT. ☹

Overnight Waking:

With toddlers, it's all about CONSEQUENCES and REWARDS. When he doesn't listen, there must be a consequence IMMEDIATELY. But if he was a good boy, the reward must also be immediate. Remember, love and affection is also a reward. It doesn't always need to be a gift.

Toddlers in a bed (>2.5 years – In a toddler bed)

<u>Just a side note:</u> You want to teach your toddler that it's not ok for him to get up overnight. Night time is for sleeping and we stay in our beds the whole night until the "sun comes up", BUT we don't want our kids to be scared to get up when there is actually something wrong. Tell him: "If you don't feel well overnight, you can come to mummy. Mummy will not consequence you"

<u>First wake up:</u>
- When your toddler wakes up, you're going to settle him the same way you did at bedtime. You're only going to sit there to support him in his learning, you're NOT there to help him.
- **If he stays in his bed and cries**, wait for 10 to 15 minutes before you respond to him at all.
- If he's still protesting after 10 to 15 minutes, go in and repeat the same strategies you were using at bedtime. Stay with him and say your key phrases until he goes back to sleep.
- Wait 5 minutes and leave.
- **If he comes to your bed**, take him straight back to his bed and give him one warning: "Michael, if you're going to get up again, Mummy is going to lock the door." Sit in the chair say your key phrases until he goes back to sleep. *(After 3 nights, no more warnings, consequence him from the first wake up)*
- Wait 5 minutes and leave.

<u>Following wake-ups:</u>
- If he gets up again, take him straight back and say: "I told you, you're not allowed to get out of your bed until the sun comes up", walk out and "lock" the door.

- Go back after 1 minute and sit in your chair, repeat the bedtime routine.
- You must repeat this same process each time he wakes in the night.
- Don't consider morning anything before 6:30 am.
- Make a big deal about it being morning and take him out of the bedroom for his first feed.

Night 4 to 6:
- Move your chair mid-room to reduce interaction. NO TOUCHING.

Night 7 to 9:
- Move your chair to the door or further away from him.

Night 10:
- Don't sit anywhere anymore. Put him down and walk out.
- If he cries longer than 10 minutes, go back into the room, say your key phrase, some careful touch and leave again.
- Repeat every 10 minutes if necessary.
- Do all this until he falls asleep.

Nap Routine:

- Tell him it's nap time
- Walk him to his room
- Change his nappy
- Bed

Toddlers in a bed (>2.5 years – In a toddler bed)

Nap
(Day 1 to 3):

- Sit beside the bed far enough away from him that he's unable to touch you.
- Say repetitive key phrases ("Night-night time" or "It's sleepy time now").
- You can occasionally touch him on the shoulder **(for 3 seconds ONLY and then lift your hand up. Don't leave your hand on his body).** We don't want this to become a new external strategy he uses to fall asleep. YOU CAN TOUCH HIM, HE ISN'T ALLOWED TO TOUCH YOU!
- If he keeps screaming, sitting up, or trying to touch you, give him one warning.
- Tell him: "If you're not going to stop screaming, sitting up, or touching Mummy, Mummy is going to leave the room and lock the door."
- If he decides to keep screaming, sitting up, or touching Mummy, stand up, walk out and close the door for only 1 minute.
- He'll get upset.
- After 1 minute, go back into the room, refer to the clock and sit in the chair. Say again: "It's sleepy time now."
- If he decides to start screaming again, walk out again but this time, close the door for 2 minutes.
- Repeat the process but increase the minutes to a **maximum** of 5 minutes.
- Try for 30 minutes only, if he hasn't slept proceed with NAP EMERGENCY

Nap Emergency:

This is how a nap emergency works:

You've tried to get your baby to sleep for 30 minutes with no success. Now, you can proceed with a NAP EMERGENCY and do whatever worked before:

- Take him for a walk in the pram
- Take him for a car ride
- Rock or pat him to sleep
- Bounce him
- Walk him to sleep in your arms
- Cuddle him in your arms
- Lay down with him

The 2 things you're NOT allowed to do:

- NO FEEDING TO SLEEP!
- NO DUMMY!

Short naps:

At this age a 1- hour nap is more than enough.

<u>If your toddler only slept for 10 minutes to 1 hour and 20 minutes:</u>
- ♥ Wait 10 minutes of full crying
- ♥ If he's still crying after 10 minutes, pick him up.

Toddlers in a bed (>2.5 years – In a toddler bed)

<u>Day 4 to 6:</u>
- ♥ Move your chair mid-room to reduce interaction. NO TOUCHING.

<u>Day 7 to 9:</u>
- ♥ Move your chair to the door, or further away from him.

<u>Day 10:</u>
- ♥ Don't sit anywhere anymore. Put him down and walk out.
- ♥ If he cries longer than 10 minutes, go back into the room, say your key phrase, some careful touch and leave again.
- ♥ Repeat every 10 minutes if necessary. Do all this until he falls asleep.

Summary:

Toddler with **1 nap:**
- **7:00 am** – Wake
- **7:30 am** – Breakfast
- **9:30 am** – Snack
- **11:00 am** – Lunch
- **12:00 pm** – Nap
- **Your toddler must be awake at 1:30 pm (depending on age and awake time)**
- **3:00 pm** – Snack
- **5:30 pm** – Dinner
- **6:30 pm** – Start his bedtime routine
- **7:00 pm** – Bedtime

Toddler with **no nap:**
- **7:00 am** – Wake
- **7:30 am** – Breakfast
- **11:00 am** - Lunch
- **12:00 – 1:00 pm** – Rest time (no nap) – NO ACTIVE PLAY
- **3:00 pm** – Snack
- **5:30 pm** – Dinner
- **6:30 pm** – Start his bedtime routine
- **7:00 pm** – Bedtime

Bedtime Routine:

- **6:30 pm** – Bath
- Dress in pyjamas

Toddlers in a bed (>2.5 years – In a toddler bed)

Milk feed + Story (keep your toddler wide awake)
7:00 pm – Bed (awake)

Bedtime:

- Sit beside the bed. Sit far enough away from him that he's unable to touch you.
- Say repetitive key phrases ("Night-night time" or "It's sleepy time now").
- If he keeps screaming, sitting up, or try to touch you, give him one warning. Tell him: "If you're not going to stop screaming, sitting up, or touching Mummy, Mummy is going to leave the room and lock the door."
- If he decides to keep screaming, sitting up, or touching mummy, stand up, walk out, and close the door for only 1 minute.
- Go back and sit next to him.
- If he decides to start screaming again, walk out again but this time you close the door for 2 minutes.
- Repeat the process but increase the minutes up to a **maximum** of 5 minutes.
- Try for 30 minutes only, if he hasn't slept proceed with NAP EMERGENCY

Overnight:

First wake-up:
- If he stays in his bed and cries, wait for 10 to 15 minutes of full crying, go in and sit.

- If he comes to your bed, take him straight back to his bed and give him one warning: "Michael, if you're going to get up again, Mummy is going to lock the door." Sit in the chair and do your **bedtime routine**.

Following wake-ups:
- If he gets up again, take him straight back, walk out and "lock" the door.
- Go back after 1 minute and sit in your chair, repeat the bedtime routine.
- You must repeat this same process each time he wakes in the night.
- Don't consider morning anything before 6:30 am.

Part 4:

General Questions and Troubleshooting

How do I go on holiday?

Travelling or going on holiday with a baby/toddler can cause a lot of stress as routine and sleep usually fly out the door. Babies and toddlers who are great sleepers at home and have a good routine going, usually adapt faster and easier to a new environment and new time zones. If you're planning a trip and you have time to prepare, I would highly recommend getting your baby/toddler in a good sleeping routine before going on holiday/travelling.

Recommendations:

- Get your baby in a good routine at least 2 weeks before travelling/going on holiday.
- Change to a travel cot 2 nights before your planned travel. I always recommend taking your own travel cot with you on holiday. Put your baby in the travel cot for ALL sleeps at least 2 days before your travel so

he can get used to it. This will lessen the impact of the new environment. Don't start co-sleeping if your baby cries a little bit the first couple of nights.
- Change to the new time zone ASAP. Depending on if you're going backward/forward in time, your baby might need an extra nap for the day, or he might skip a nap. It's very important to follow your normal awake times between naps and bedtime. It's also important to follow your normal routine at bedtime so your baby can recognise all the sleep cues. On the first morning, follow your normal routine at the local time.
- Choose the right travel gear, it will certainly help smooth the journey. A baby sling/carrier will make it easier on buses and trains, it also keeps your hands free if you need your passport or to pay for things.
- I always recommend taking travel blackout blinds (like the GRO blinds). Your baby's sleep will be a lot better if the room is dark.
- Never forget your baby's favourite toys and comforter.
- At your destination, try to get organised as soon as possible. Set up the room to make it as close to home as possible. Settling in will help you remain organised (and sane) throughout your stay.
- Stick to your normal routine and rules. Don't bend the rules just because you're on holiday:
    - ♥ No TV/iPad before bed
    - ♥ No co-sleeping
    - ♥ Try to eat as normal as possible (babies get upset tummies very easily)
    - ♥ Don't give your toddler extra sugar (lollies)

How do I go on holiday?

- ♥ Bedtime is bedtime. If bedtime is 7 pm at home, it's 7 pm on your holiday. You're very busy and active on your holiday, your baby/toddler needs more sleep than at home, not less.
- ♥ Never over-schedule your holiday. When your baby is overstimulated and can't have proper naps in a cot, he's going to become overtired and very cranky (not a good recipe for a nice relaxing holiday!). Try to organise day trips after the morning nap (which is usually the best nap) and the second nap can be in a pram/car.

Travelling by car/flying:

- Try to travel at night if possible. It's easier if the baby/toddler can sleep most of the time.
- Get a new special toy or colouring books. Something exciting and new that can keep him occupied for a while.
- If possible, financially, pay for a seat for your baby/toddler even if they're under the age of one. Otherwise, you can end up very cramped on a full flight with a baby on your lap. Not to mention that you can't fold your table down, which means mealtimes can be difficult.
- Have exciting snacks for the trip. Exciting food always keeps them occupied for a while. Don't give everything at once, it might lead to cramps or vomiting.

It might be very scary to travel with your child but the more you practice, the better your child will become at travelling.

I want to visit friends and go to a restaurant
Yes, life goes on. Please go out and enjoy life, but please go prepared. If you know you're going to be at a restaurant or friend's place when it's time for your baby's nap or bedtime, prepare for that sleep. A nap can happen in a pram or your arms if it's only going to happen on occasion. If you're going to have bedtime at a restaurant or friend's house, have a mini version of your bedtime routine. Just a quick cream rub, PJ's, milk, sleeping bag, and then in the pram or a porta cot. You can't stretch your baby to be awake longer than they can handle.

My baby is sick, what do I do?
If he's sick, wait 2 to 3 minutes when he's crying instead of 10 minutes and respond to his calls. Give him some comfort and then put him back into bed to drift off to sleep on his own again. Please don't start to feed him again or rock him to sleep because he's sick. It isn't needed. Your baby has a perfect skill now to sleep. Don't ruin it now because you THINK he needs it. Does someone rock or pat you to sleep when you're sick? NO. Please don't do it.

I don't want to stay at home all the time
You don't have to. Sleeps in the pram, the car or in your arms are allowed if it only happens on occasions. Life goes on, I honestly don't expect you to stay at home all the time. Just prepare for the sleep.

Early morning wake-ups
This can be a difficult one, especially at the beginning of sleep training. Suddenly, your baby is getting more sleep than normal and when he wakes up at 5 am, he feels brilliant. How you're going to respond at 5 am depends on how old your baby is. If you have a small baby and it has been 3 or 4 hours, you'll feed your baby at 5/6 am and allow him to go back to sleep. Remember, you'll feed him again at 7 am to restart the day's feeding schedule. If your baby is 7 months and older, he isn't supposed to have a feed so you must resettle your baby.

- Wait 10 minutes of full crying. Just think during this time about whether your baby is teething and if he still has enough pain relief in his body. If he doesn't,

get the medication and give it to him as soon as you walk in. Most parents forget this one.
- Go in, check that he's ok but don't give him ANY attention. They, unfortunately, wake up for the 5 am attention.
- Walk out.
- Wait 10 minutes of full crying.
- Go in and check or you can just watch him on the monitor because you know he's ok. At 5 am, it can be difficult to go back to sleep because we all have very light sleep.
- Repeat until he goes back to sleep. Even if it takes an hour or 2.

DON'T:

- Put him in your bed
- Pick him up (unless you've to change a nappy or think something might be wrong)
- Give him a feed if he isn't supposed to have a feed
- Start rocking and patting him to sleep
- Lay down with him
- Start staying in the room

Day-care

Starting day-care or going back to day-care can cause a bit of anxiety for a parent, especially if your baby is now a brilliant sleeper at home. Going to day-care can be an adjustment for your baby/toddler. Please give him time to adjust.

How do I go on holiday?

A few things you can do to help with the adjustment:

- Give your day-care the nap part of your plan and ask them if they can follow that
- Please remove all dummies from your baby's day-care bag
- Ask the person at day-care not to sit down next to your baby when he falls asleep because they'll pat or stroke him to sleep
- If your baby is still in a cot at day-care, don't forget the sleeping bag/swaddle
- Don't forget your baby's comforter
- If your baby is sensitive to noise, you can give the day-care a mobile white noise machine to try and block out the other babies' cries
- Day-care is busy, your baby will be more tired. Please put him down earlier at night. My kids went to bed at 6 pm on day-care days and slept 13 hours!!! Please don't be scared to ever put your child down earlier

When do I move my toddler from a cot to a toddler bed?

I don't move toddlers out of their cots before the age of **2.5 years,** but I prefer closer to 3 years. Before 2.5 years, most toddlers don't understand: "I'm in a big boy bed and I'm not allowed to get out, if I get out when nothing is wrong, there will be a consequence." If your child keeps getting up overnight, even if you keep putting him back, he really doesn't understand. He isn't ready to be in a toddler bed.

You can move 2.5-year-old toddlers who have been good sleepers into a toddler bed because they're already sleep trained and they sleep through the night, but sleep training a 2.5-year-old in a toddler bed is very difficult. Initially, there will be a "honeymoon phase" which lasts up to a month and then the trouble starts. If your child is still happy in the cot, please don't move him out.

How to keep my 2- to 2.5-year-old in the cot?

I get this all the time: "I moved my 2-year-old into a toddler bed because he kept climbing out of the cot." A 2-year-old isn't ready to be in a toddler bed. Put him back into the cot and get creative to keep him inside.

A few tricks:

- Put him back into a sleeping bag (the bag one not the one with the separated legs. Most toddlers are then unable to lift their legs high enough to jump out. If your child keeps getting out of the sleeping bag, have the sleeping bag:
  - Inside-out
  - Front-to-back (Zip or buttons on the back)

How do I go on holiday?

- If you have a cot where the back is higher than the front, turn the cot around so the higher part of the cot is at the front.

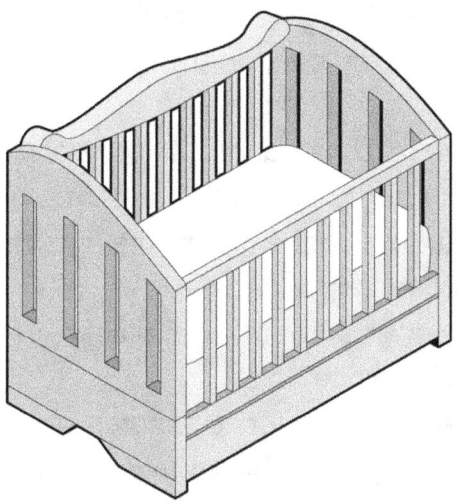

- Take the base of the cot out and put the mattress on the floor. It will look like a playpen. You win the height where the base was.

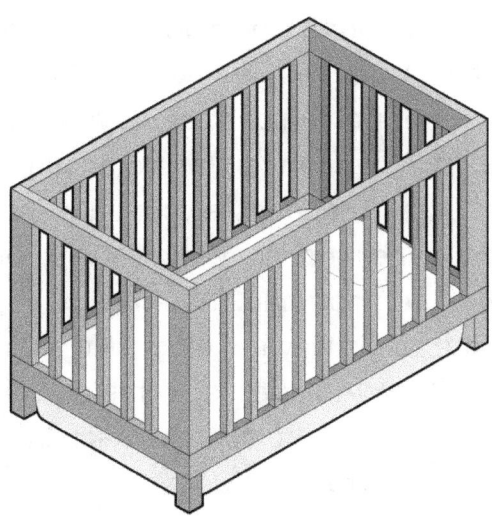

When and how to move from 3 naps to 2?

Usually, babies move from 3 naps to 2 naps around the age of 6.5 to 7 months. A baby's awake time at this age is usually around 2.5 to 3 hours which means your baby must be awake at around 4 pm to be tired enough to go to bed at 7 pm. If it gets too difficult, do the following:

- Skip the third nap and put your baby down at 6 pm
- Stretch your baby a little longer before the 1st and 2nd nap to balance the awake time during the day
- Encourage longer naps:
    - Have the room pitch black
    - Use white noise
    - Always wait for 10 minutes of crying before you pick your baby up from the nap to give your baby an opportunity to resettle and go back to sleep independently

When and how to move from 2 naps to 1?

Usually, babies move from 2 naps to 1 nap around the age of 13 to 14 months. A baby's awake time at this age is usually around 4 to 4.5 hours which means your baby must be awake at around 2:30/3 pm to be tired enough to go to bed at 7 pm. What usually happens is your baby will go down for his normal nap in the morning around 10/10:30 am but then he refuses the afternoon nap. This means his awake time at the end of the day is way too much. He gets so tired and grumpy around 5 pm, temper tantrums can happen, or he wants a nap at 5 pm. If he continues to skip the 2nd nap and you think your baby is ready to go to 1 nap, do the following:

How do I go on holiday?

- Stretch your baby's first nap to 11 am. Please don't put him down before 11 am.
- Put him down at 6 pm for the night.
- It will take him approximately 4 weeks to adjust to having only 1 nap.
    - Week 0: Nap at 11 am
      Bedtime at 6 pm
    - Week 1: Nap at 11:15 am
      Bedtime at 6:15 pm
    - Week 2: Nap at 11:30 am
      Bedtime at 6:30 pm
    - Week 3: Nap at 11:45 am
      Bedtime at 6:45 pm
    - Week 4: Nap at 12 pm
      Bedtime at 7 pm

When and how to move from 1 nap to none?

Your baby is on 1 nap now and I want you to treat the nap as an onion. You're going to peel off the skin on both ends until only 30 minutes is left of the nap. You always wake your baby at 7 am and you always put him down at 7 pm. The general rule is, if your baby doesn't fall asleep within less than 10 minutes (not because of teething) he needs more **awake time** because he's growing older. If you struggle to put your baby down for a nap, you give him more awake time which means you put him down later for the nap. Instead of 12 pm, you put him down at 12:15 pm.

If you struggle to put your baby down at 7 pm, he needs more awake time in the afternoon. Wake him up from the nap earlier. Instead of waking him up at 2 pm, you wake him at

1:45 pm. On both ends, the nap will get shorter and shorter. A nap of 30 minutes is still considered a nap. If your baby is having a 30-minute nap and you're still struggling to get him down for the nap or get him down at night, it might be time to cut the nap. Please don't cut the nap before the age of 2.5 years. They do go through a nap regression at 2 years. Please persist. Your child isn't ready to cut the nap.

If you think your child is ready to cut the nap do the following:

- Give your child a "rest time" from 12 to 1 pm. In this time, give your child quiet time. NO active play. Your child can watch a movie, play with Lego, build a puzzle, read a book. It doesn't matter but NO SLEEP.

- Put your child down at 6 pm for sleep. Bedtime routine at 5:30 pm. It will take your child 4 weeks to adjust to having no nap.

Milestones to look out for.
Don't focus too much on "The Wonder Weeks" (The "Wonder Weeks" are the ten leaps in mental development that every child goes through in their first twenty months of life) because it's very specific to what is happening to your baby in a certain week. Every baby is different, and they develop at their own pace. If you follow the wonder weeks very strictly, you might miss when your baby is genuinely unwell.

Babies are growing very fast during their first year of life. There is physical growth (height and weight) but also developmental milestones. Developmental milestones are the skills your baby starts mastering like rolling, sitting, and walking.

Babies tend to follow the same progression throughout these milestones. But remember, every baby is different which means the type and length of the stages can be different. It's good to know what to expect, approximately when to expect it, and how to manage it. It decreases the stress and anxiety around it.

Month 1
During the first month of life, most babies' behaviours are reflexive. Everything happens automatically. There are 4 main reflexes:

1. Mouthing reflex
   - Sucking and swallowing reflex. A baby will automatically begin to suck when their mouth or lips are touched.
   - Rooting reflex. A baby will automatically turn his head towards your hand if their cheek is touched. This fades at 4 months.

These reflexes are very important for a baby's survival and to help them to find food.

2. Startle (Moro) reflex
This reflex occurs when a baby hears a loud noise or when he falls backward. His arms and legs extend away from his body. The startle reflex will keep waking your baby when he sleeps. To improve sleep, you must swaddle your baby. Initially, your baby might not like it, but it's important to persist to improve sleep. This fades at 4 months.

3. Grasp reflex
A baby will automatically grab a finger or object when it's placed in the palm of his hand. This fades at 5 months.

4. Stepping reflex
When a baby is placed with his feet on a flat surface, he'll automatically step one foot in front of the other. This fades around 2 months.

1 to 3 months
- More aware of their surroundings
- Follow moving objects
- Starts smiling at familiar faces
- Can hold his head up for a few seconds when on his tummy
- Open and shuts hands
- Grab and shakes hand toys
- Pushes legs down when on a flat surface
- Make cooing sounds

4 to 7 months
- Starts coordinating vision, touch, and hearing
- Starts rolling (stop swaddling)
- Starts sitting up
- Some may start crawling
- Starts pushing up by using their arms and arching their back to lift the chest. These movements strengthen the upper body, preparing the body for sitting up
- Rocking while on his stomach
- Kicking legs
- Bringing toys to their mouths

How do I go on holiday?

- Discovering feet and toes
- Like looking at themselves in the mirror
- Transfers objects from one hand to the other hand
- Laughs
- Babbles

8 to 12 months
- Sit without support
- Starts crawling (7 to 8 months)
- Very mobile—like exploring (very important to childproof your house, especially the kitchen and bathroom)
- Starts standing (around 9 to 10 months)
- First step around 12 months
- Like to poke their fingers through holes (remember to cover all power points)
- Usually, the first word at 12 months
- Separation anxiety and stranger anxiety can start at this point

By the end of this period:
- Gets in and out of sitting position independently
- Gets in hand and knees position and crawls
- Pulls himself up to a standing position
- Walks holding on to furniture
- Stands without support
- Eventually takes a few steps without support and begins to walk
- Uses pincer grasp (thumb and first finger)
- Places objects into containers and takes them out
- More functional activities like holding a spoon and turning pages in a book

Toddler
Sits alone – 5 to 9 months
Crawls – 6 to 12 months
Stands – 8 to 17 months
Walks alone – 9 to 18 months
First words – 1 to 3 years
2-word phrases – 15 to 32 months
Responsive smile – 1 to 3 months
Finger feeds – 7 to 14 months
Drinks from cup unassisted – 9 to 17 months
Uses spoon – 12 to 20 months
Bowel control – 16 to 42 months
Dresses self-unassisted – 3.25 to 5 years

Constipation

Constipation can be very painful, and it affects sleep. Try to avoid it at all costs. Treat it as soon as possible.

In babies, constipation refers to hard bowel motions, not infrequent bowel motions. Babies may have several bowel motions per day, which is normal, or one every second or third day, which is also normal. The most common cause for constipation is when a baby/toddler associate passing a stool with pain, so they delay toileting, and the problem gets worse. It's quite rare for breastfed babies to be constipated. It usually starts when:

- You start introducing solids
- You start introducing formula

How do I go on holiday?

- When your baby isn't getting enough fluids in their diet.

The most common signs of constipation are:

- The poo is hard, dry, or crumbly and looks like marbles. You can use the Bristol Stool Chart to assess it
- Your baby is crying and looks uncomfortable before doing a poo
- The poo or wind smells bad
- Your baby isn't eating enough
- Your baby has a hard belly
- If the poo is very hard, it can sometimes cause small tears around your baby's anus (back passage). These little tears can bleed and cause more pain and discomfort

BRISTOL STOOL CHART

	TYPE 1	Seperated hard lumps	Very Constipated
	TYPE 2	Lumpy and sausage like	Slightly Constipated
	TYPE 3	A sausage shape with crads in the surface	Normal
	TYPE 4	Like a smoth, soft suasage or snake	Normal
	TYPE 5	Soft blobs with clear-cut edge	Lacking Fibre
	TYPE 6	Mushy consistency with ragged edges	Inflammation
	TYPE 7	Liquid Consistency with no solid pieces	Inflammation

What to do:
- Never give your baby medication for constipation unless prescribed by your doctor.
- *Breastfed babies:* Feed your baby more often. See your doctor.
- *Formula-fed babies*: Make sure the formula has been made correctly (enough water). Make sure you're adding water to the bottle first, then the formula powder.
- *Solid fed babies*: Offer water/diluted fruit juice (especially prune juice) between meals (1 part juice to 3 parts water). Encourage your baby/toddler to eat more fruit and vegetables. Many different foods can contribute to constipation. Too much applesauce, bananas, and cereal (especially rice cereal).

Other things you can do:
- Gently move your baby's legs in a cycling motion—this may help stimulate their bowel.
- Gently massage your baby's tummy.
- **Gentle** rectal stimulation with the use of a cotton swab or rectal thermometer.
- Glycerine suppository.
- Encourage your toilet-trained child to develop the habit of sitting on the toilet regularly and pushing. 2 times a day for 3 to 5 minutes each time. Try this 20 to 30 minute after meals.
- It can help if your child has a footstool/box.

If your baby is constipated, try to get this under control before thinking of doing sleep training. It's very difficult to sleep train a constipated baby.

How do I go on holiday?

Reflux

Infant reflux occurs when the muscles between the oesophagus and the stomach relax, and the baby spits up a little bit or vomits a lot. This usually happens after a feed. The following steps can help to improve the vomiting:

- Follow an eat-play-sleep routine which means your baby's milk feeds will always be fed AFTER sleep, not before
- Keep your baby upright during a feed
- Don't allow your baby to "scull down" his milk. Give a break after a few minutes of drinking
- Burp your baby often during a feed
- Lift your baby's cot feed on an angle so your baby isn't flat in the cot. Only do this if your baby has no linen in the cot (swaddled or sleeping bag only)
- See your GP, your baby might need medication

Is it normal for my baby to be so clingy?

Starting a new routine and doing sleep training is a big change for your baby. He has no clue what is going on. They're usually a bit clingier at the start, but it improves when they get more familiar with the routine and feel more rested.

When your body is used to getting 6 hours of sleep and on a Saturday, you get 8 or 9 hours, you actually feel worse. It feels like your head is in a cloud. That's how your baby feels when he suddenly starts to get a lot more sleep. Give your baby's body time to adjust to the new amount of sleep. ☺

My baby cries as soon as I put him down on the changing table to change his nappy, is that normal?

Yes, it can be normal. You can put a musical mobile on your changing table to try and distract your baby.

My baby is still tired when I wake him from his last nap, can I let him sleep longer?

If he hasn't slept his 20 minutes yet, yes let him sleep until he has had 20 minutes, then wake him up. But if he has had his 20 minutes, please wake him. If letting him sleep longer is going to mean going to bed later at night, please don't do it. The uninterrupted overnight sleep means more for your baby's rest, healing, and growing than longer naps during the day. Please try to keep with the 12 hours overnight as close as possible.

Do I have to wake my baby up at 7:00 am or can I let him sleep in?

Your baby needs 12 hours during the day to fit in all his naps and food and your baby needs 12 hours overnight for sleep. If you don't wake your baby at 7 am, it's ok but that will mean a later bedtime. It's ok to follow a 7:30 am – 7:30 pm or an 8 am – 8 pm schedule.

My baby wakes up multiple times overnight, cries for a few minutes, and then goes back to sleep, is that normal?

If you don't have to go in at all since, he self-settles every time, yes, it's fine. He's going from 1 sleep cycle to another, he's just a bit more vocal than you are about it. He's ok. If you think he might be teething and the teething keeps him up, go in, give a dose of medication, and walk out.

My baby takes 20 to 30 minutes to go to sleep, why is that?

He might not be tired enough, give him 10 or 20 minutes more awake time. Or he might be teething. Give him Nurofen 30 minutes before you put him down for sleep.

If I gave Nurofen/Panadol at bedtime, do I have to give it again overnight?

If your baby is teething, absolutely YES! Pain medication only lasts for 4 to 6 hours. If your baby wakes up screaming at 1 am, he's in pain. There is no pain medication in his body. Give him something for pain. Nurofen is always the drug of choice for teething because it's an anti-inflammatory.

I have already given Nurofen for 3 days, shouldn't I stop it?

It depends on if you only gave it for 3 days at night-time or did you give it for 3 days every 4 to 6 hours? Mix it up with Panadol to have a better effect. The problem is your baby is in pain. You can't let your baby just cry in pain because you want to stop the medication. If you think you're giving too much medication and your baby is still in pain, go and see your GP.

Will the crying harm my baby or break the bond between us?

If he's crying because you're sleep training and you're teaching your baby a sleep skill, absolutely not. The crying is short-lived anyway. As soon as your baby has the skills and has caught up with sleep, the crying will be less and every day.

Happy Sleepers

Will my baby still love me?
Absolutely YES!!!!

Happy Sleepers Program Checklists

Problem	Solution
Baby keeps crying for naps and bedtime • Is my baby tired enough? • Is my baby overtired? • Is my baby teething? • Does my baby need pain relief?	• Next time give more awake time • Next time give less awake time • Give Nurofen/Panadol and SM33 • Give pain relief
My baby keeps on crying overnight • Is my baby teething? • Did my baby have a good feed at bedtime? • Did my baby have screentime before bed?	• Give Nurofen/Panadol and SM33 • Keep your baby fully awake for bedtime feed. This feed is very important • No screentime 1 - 2 hours before bed
My baby keeps waking up early • Any noise at that time of the morning? • Is my baby teething? • Is my baby hungry? • Is my baby cold? • Is the room still pitch black? (summer)	• Use white noise (12 hours) • Give top-up pain medication and gel • Only give a feed if your baby is younger than 6.5 months. Give a proper bedtime feed. • Dress warmer at bedtime. Warm up the room. • Improve darkness in the room.

How do I go on holiday?

Happy Sleepers Program Checklists

Problem | Solution

Short naps
- Did my baby fall asleep in the cot, not in my arms?
- Any noises waking my baby?
- Is the room pitch black?
- Is my baby teething?
- Is my baby hungry?
- Am I waiting 10 min of full crying?

Solution:
- Your baby must be fully awake in the cot, NOT drowsy or half asleep.
- Use white noise
- Make the room darker
- Give pain medication and gel
- Have a structured 4 hourly feeding routine
- Wait 10 min of full on crying to allow resetting.

Is my baby teething?
- Is my baby chewing on everything?
- Does my baby have red cheeks?
- Are the gums swollen?
- Is my baby drooling a lot?

Solution:
- Give Nurofen every 3 hours (if needed)
- Give Panadol every 3 hours (if needed)
- Apply SM33 gel
- Give icy pole
- Put teething rings in freezer
- Give teething rusks

My baby has a cold
- Is my baby coughing?
- Does my baby have a runny nose?
- Does my baby sound congested?
- Does my baby have a fever?

Solution:
- A warm humidifier in your baby's room for all naps and bedtime
- Warm humidifier and use a nasal aspirator
- Warm humidifier
- Panadol, undress, give a cold washdown
- When ever concerned ALWAYS consult your GP

Happy Sleepers

	You are my Sunshine	Ring a Ring a Rosie	Old McDonald had a Farm	Super Trooper
	DIY video training (Available Worldwide)	Zoom Consultation	Half night (Virtual) (Australia)	1x Full night (Virtual) (6pm-6am) (Australia)
	14 Day Sleep Plan + Training Videos	14 Day Sleep Plan + Training Videos	14 Day Sleep Plan + Training Videos	14 Day Sleep Plan + Training Videos
	5x Consultation Videos	30 min Zoom Consultation for Q & A	30 min Zoom Consultation for Q & A	30 min Zoom Consultation for Q & A
	Night 1: Video Support	Night 1: SMS support until baby sleeps	Night 1: Virtual support via a 4G camera for 6 hours (6:30 pm - 12:30 am)	Night 1: Virtual support via a 4G camera for 12 hours (6:30 pm - 6:30 am)
	14 Days of Video Support	14 Days of Telephone Support	14 Days of Telephone Support	14 Days of Telephone Support
	Twins video	+ $100	+ $150	+ $150
	IMMEDIATE ACCESS	HELP ASAP, MINIMUM WAIT	GOOD BALANCE	BEST VALUE

Notes

www.ingramcontent.com/pod-product-compliance
Lightning Source LLC
Chambersburg PA
CBHW071606080526
44588CB00010B/1041